Praise for *The Cost of Rights*

"With an argument elegant in its simplicity, the authors have profoundly changed the debate over rights. . . . This book helps establish a far more credible and realistic approach to dealing with some of the most vexing matters in the body politic."
—Thomas Byrne Edsall, author of *Chain Reaction: The Impact of Race, Rights, and Taxes on American Politics*

"Holmes and Sunstein offer a powerful challenge of liberal and conservative shibboleths about the distinction between negative and positive liberty. This subtle and wide-ranging book casts new light on the debate about the appropriate boundaries of the regulatory state."
—Jeffrey Rose, legal affairs editor, *The New Republic*

"A brilliant and refreshing look into the conditions necessary for the protection of rights, *The Cost of Rights* is essential to understanding how individual liberty depends fundamentally on social cooperation and government action."
—George Soros, chairman and founder of the Open Society Institute and author of *The Crises of Global Capitalism*

"A compelling analysis of the intellectual failures of libertarianism and a much-needed appeal for a better kind of liberalism."
—Bruce Ackerman, Sterling Professor of Law and Political Science, Yale University

"[The authors] take on a slew of American prejudices and, by demolishing them, demonstrate the considerable resources of the sort of middle of the road liberalism that has recently been thought to be either dead or on the defensive. . . . The great virtue of *The Cost of Rights* is a highly developed common sense."

—Alan Ryan, Oxford University

"*The Cost of Rights* will be an eye-opener for many. When you read Holmes and Sunstein's book, you will be stunned, surprised, and convinced, and will see many familiar facts in a new light. Crisp, crystal clear, and studded with vivid examples, *The Cost of Rights* is that rare book, an 'instant classic.'"

—Jon Elster, Columbia University

THE COST OF RIGHTS

ALSO BY STEPHEN HOLMES

Passions and Constraint
Anatomy of Antiliberalism
Benjamin Constant and the Making of Modern Liberalism

ALSO BY CASS R. SUNSTEIN

Free Markets and Social Justice
Legal Reasoning and Political Conflict
The Partial Constitution
After the Rights Revolution
Democracy and the Problem of Free Speech
One Case at a Time: Judicial Minimalism on the Supreme Court

THE COST
OF RIGHTS

Why Liberty Depends on Taxes

STEPHEN HOLMES
AND CASS R. SUNSTEIN

W. W. Norton & Company
New York • London

TO GEOFFREY STONE

For information about permission to reproduce selections from this book, write
to Permissions, W. W. Norton & Company, Inc., 500 Fifth Avenue, New York,
NY 10110.

The text of this book is composed in Garamond No. 3
with the display set in Fenice
Desktop composition by Chelsea Dippel
Manufacturing by Quebecor Printing, Fairfield, Inc.
Book design by BTD

LIBRARY OF CONGRESS CATALOGING-IN-PUBLICATION DATA
Holmes, Stephen, 1948–
The cost of rights : why liberty depends on taxes / Stephen Holmes and
Cass R. Sunstein.
p. cm.
Includes bibliographical references and index.
ISBN 0-393-04670-2
1. Civil rights—United States—Costs. 2. Finance, Public—United States.
3. Government spending policy—United States. I. Sunstein, Cass R. II. Title.
JC599.U5 H55 1999
323'0973—dc21   98-41491
                                                                    CIP

ISBN 0-393-32033-2 pbk.

W. W. Norton & Company, Inc., 500 Fifth Avenue, New York, N.Y. 10110
www.wwnorton.com

W. W. Norton & Company Ltd., 10 Coptic Street, London WC1A 1PU

4 5 6 7 8 9 0

CONTENTS

PART IV:
UNDERSTANDING RIGHTS AS BARGAINS

CONCLUSION:
THE PUBLIC CHARACTER OF PRIVATE FREEDOMS

APPENDIX:
SOME NUMBERS ON RIGHTS AND THEIR COSTS

NOTES

INDEX

ACKNOWLEDGMENTS

IT IS A KEEN PLEASURE to thank the many friends and colleagues who helped us with this book. We first stumbled across the cost of rights, as a subject for inquiry and analysis, in discussions at the Center on Constitutionalism in Eastern Europe at the University of Chicago. A healthy respect for the fiscal preconditions of effective rights enforcement arose naturally from observing the underprotection of basic liberties in the insolvent states of Eastern Europe and the former Soviet Union. Russia's great experiment with the jury trial, to choose a typical example, went awry when it began to consume 25 percent of already inadequate local court budgets. One of our principal goals here has been to apply what we learned in this eye-opening context to the debate about rights underway in the United States. We thank Dwight Semler, the coordinator of the Center, and our co-directors, Jon Elster, Larry Lessig, and Wiktor Osiatynski, as well as Andras Sajo, for many challenging discussions. We are also grateful for searching criticisms and wily suggestions on the manuscript from Elster, Bruce Ackerman, Samuel Beer, Martin Krygier, Martha Nussbaum, Richard Posner, and Bernard Yack. Sophie Clark, Keith Sharfman, Matthew Utterbeck, and Christian Lucky provided invaluable research assistance. Appreciation also goes to our editor, Alane Salierno Mason, for her incisive comments and steady encouragement.

THE COST OF RIGHTS

Introduction:
COMMON SENSE ABOUT RIGHTS

ON AUGUST 26, 1995, a fire broke out in Westhampton, on the westernmost edge of the celebrated Long Island Hamptons, one of the most beautiful areas in the United States. This fire was the worst experienced by New York in the past half-century. For thirty-six hours it raged uncontrollably, at one point measuring six miles by twelve.

But this story has a happy ending. In a remarkably short time, local, state, and federal forces moved in to quell the blaze. Officials and employees from all levels of government descended upon the scene. More than fifteen hundred local volunteer firefighters joined with military and civilian teams from across the state and country. Eventually, the fire was brought under control. Astonishingly, no one was killed. Equally remarkably, destruction of property was minimal. Volunteerism helped, but in the end, public resources made this rescue possible. Ultimate costs to American taxpayers, local and national, originally estimated at $1.1 million, may have been as high as $2.9 million.

Opposition to government has been a defining theme of American populism in the late twentieth century. Its slogan is, Don't tread on me! Or as Ronald Reagan put it, "Government isn't the solution; it's the problem." More recently, critics of all things governmental, such as Charles Murray and David Boaz, have claimed that an "adult making an honest living and mind-ing his own business deserves to be left alone," and that the "real problem in the United States is the same one being recognized all over the world: too much government."[1]

Yet in Westhampton, on the spur of the moment, public officials were able to organize and direct a costly and collective effort to defend private property, drawing liberally on public resources contributed by the citizenry at large, for the emergency rescue of real estate owned by a relatively small number of wealthy families.

There is nothing exceptional about this story. In 1996, American taxpayers devoted at least $11.6 billion to protecting private property by means of disaster relief and disaster insurance.[2] Every day, every hour, private catastrophes are averted or mitigated by public expenditures that are sometimes large, even massive, but that often go unrecognized. Americans simply assume that our public officials—national, state, and local—will routinely lay hold of public resources and expend them to salvage, or boost the value of, private rights. Despite the undesirably high incidence of crime in the United States, for instance, a majority of citizens feel relatively secure most of the time, in good measure due to the efforts of the police, publicly salaried protectors of one of our most basic liberties: personal or physical security.[3]

Public support for the kind of "safety net" that benefited the home owners of Westhampton is broad and deep, but at the same time, Americans seem easily to forget that individual rights and freedoms depend fundamentally on vigorous state action. Without effective government, American citizens would not be able to enjoy their private property in the way they do. Indeed, they would enjoy few or none of their constitutionally guaranteed individual rights. Personal liberty, as Americans value and experience it, presupposes social cooperation managed by government officials. The private realm we rightly prize is sustained, indeed created, by public action. Not even the most self-reliant citizen is asked to look after his or her material welfare autonomously, without any support from fellow citizens or public officials.

The story of the Westhampton fire is the story of property ownership across America and, in truth, throughout the world. Indeed, it is the story of all liberal rights. When structured constitutionally and made (relatively speaking) democratically responsive, government is an indispensable device for mobilizing and channeling effectively the diffuse resources of the community, bringing them to bear on problems, in pinpoint operations, whenever these unexpectedly flare up.

The Declaration of Independence states that "to secure these rights, Governments are established among men." To the obvious truth that rights depend on government must be added a logical corollary, one rich with implications: rights cost money. Rights cannot be protected or enforced without public funding and support. This is just as true of old rights as of new rights, of the rights of Americans before as well as after Franklin Delano Roosevelt's New Deal. Both the right to welfare and the right to private property have public costs. The right to freedom of contract has public costs no less than the right to health care, the right to freedom of speech no less than the right to decent housing. All rights make claims upon the public treasury.

The "cost of rights" is a richly ambiguous phrase because both words have multiple and inevitably controversial meanings. To keep the analysis as focused and, along this dimension, as uncontentious as possible, "costs" will be understood here to mean *budgetary costs* and "rights" will be defined as *important interests that can be reliably protected by individuals or groups using the instrumentalities of government.* Both definitions require elaboration.

DEFINING RIGHTS

The term "rights" has many referents and shades of meaning. There are, broadly speaking, two distinct ways to approach the subject: moral and descriptive. The first associates rights with moral principles or ideals. It identifies rights not by consulting statutes and case law, but by asking what human beings are morally entitled to. While no single agreed-upon theory of such moral rights exists, some of the most interesting philosophical work on rights involves an ethical inquiry, evaluative in nature, of this general kind. Moral philosophy conceives of nonlegal rights as moral claims of the strongest sort, enjoyed perhaps by virtue of one's status or capacity as a moral agent, not as a result of one's membership in, or legal relationship to, a particular political society. The moral account of rights tries to identify those human interests that may not, before the tribunal of conscience, ever be neglected or intruded upon without special justification.

A second approach to rights—with roots in the writings of the British philosopher Jeremy Bentham, American Supreme Court Justice Oliver Wendell Holmes, Jr., and legal philosophers Hans Kelsen and H. L. A. Hart—is more descriptive and less evaluative. It is more interested in explaining how legal systems actually function and less oriented toward justification. It is not a moral account.[4] It takes no stand on which human interests are, from a philosophical perspective, the most important and worthy. It neither affirms nor denies ethical skepticism and moral relativism. Instead it is an empirical inquiry into the kinds of interests that a particular politically organized society actually protects. Within this framework, an interest qualifies as a right when an effective legal system treats it as such by using collective resources to defend it. As a capacity created and maintained by the state to restrain or redress harm, a right in the legal sense is, by definition, a "child of the law."

Rights in the legal sense have "teeth." They are therefore anything but harmless or innocent. Under American law, rights are powers granted by the political community. And like the wielder of any other power, an individual who exercises his or her rights may be tempted to use them badly. The right of one individual to sue another is the classic example. Because a right implies a power that can be wielded, for good or ill, over others, it must be guarded against and restricted, even while being scrupulously protected. Freedom of speech itself must be trimmed when its misuse (such as shouting "Fire!" in a crowded theater) endangers public safety. A rights-based political regime would dissolve into mutually destructive and self-defeating chaos without well-designed and carefully upheld protections against the *misuse* of basic rights.

When they are not backed by legal force, by contrast, moral rights are toothless by definition. Unenforced moral rights are aspirations binding on conscience, not powers binding on officials. They impose moral duties on all mankind, not legal obligations on the inhabitants of a territorially bounded nation-state. Because legally unrecognized moral rights are untainted by power, they can be advocated freely without much worry about malicious misuse, perverse incentives, and unintended side effects. Rights under law invariably raise such misgivings and concerns.

For most purposes, moral and positive accounts of rights need not be at odds. Advocates of moral rights and describers of legal rights simply have different agendas. The moral theorist might reasonably say that, in the abstract, there is no "right to pollute." But the positivist knows that, in American jurisdictions, an upstream landowner can acquire a right to pollute a river from a downstream landowner. The points are not contradictory, but simply pass each other in the night. Those who offer moral accounts and those who offer positive accounts are asking and answering different questions. So students of collectively enforceable rights have no quarrel with those who offer moral arguments on behalf of one or another right or understanding of rights. Legal reformers should obviously strive to align politically enforceable rights with what seems to them to be morally right. And those charged with enforcing legal rights would do well to convince the public that these rights are morally well founded.

But the cost of rights is in the first instance a descriptive, not a moral, theme. Moral rights have budgetary costs only if their precise nature and scope are politically stipulated and interpreted—that is, only if they are recognizable under law. True, the cost of rights can be morally relevant, for a theory of rights that never descends from the heights of morality into the world of scarce resources will be sorely incomplete, even from a moral perspective. Since "ought implies can," and lack of resources implies cannot, moral theorists should probably pay more attention than they usually do to taxing and spending. And they cannot fully explore the moral dimensions of rights protection if they fail to consider the question of distributive justice. After all, collectively provided resources are often, for no good reason, channeled to secure the rights of some citizens rather than the rights of others.

Rights are ordinarily enforced in functioning and adequately funded courts of law. Not included among the rights discussed in this book, therefore, are rights such as those of women raped in war zones of Bosnia or Rwanda. Existing political authorities have in effect turned their backs on the sickeningly brutal wrongs perpetrated under such conditions, claiming that such crimes do not fall under their jurisdictions. Precisely because remedial authorities universally shrug them off, such miserably neglected "rights" have no direct budgetary costs. In the absence of a political authority that is willing and able to intervene, rights remain a hollow promise and, at present, place no burdens on any public treasury.

Not even the ostensibly legal rights guaranteed under international human rights declarations and covenants will be discussed here unless subscribing national states—capable of taxing and spending—reliably support international tribunals, such as those in Strasbourg or the Hague, where genuine redress can be sought when such rights are violated. In practice, rights become more than mere declarations only if they confer power on bodies whose decisions are legally binding (as the moral rights announced in the United Nations Declaration of Human Rights of 1948, for example, do not). As a general rule, unfortunate individuals who do not live under a government capable of taxing and delivering an effective remedy[5] have no legal rights. Statelessness spells rightslessness. A legal right exists, in reality, only when and if it has budgetary costs.

Because this book focuses exclusively on rights that are enforceable by politically organized communities, it pays no attention to many moral claims of great importance to the liberal tradition. This regrettable loss of scope can be justified by an enhanced clarity of focus. Even if legally unenforceable rights are put to one side, enough difficult problems remain to occupy our attention.

Philosophers also distinguish between liberty and the value of liberty. Liberty has little value if those who ostensibly possess it lack the resources to make their rights effective. Freedom to hire a lawyer means little if all lawyers charge fees, if the state will not help, and if you have no money. The right to private property, an important part of liberty, means little if you lack the resources to protect what you own and the police are unavailable. Only liberties that are valuable in practice lend legitimacy to a liberal political order. This book does not focus exclusively on the budgetary costs of rights that are enforceable in courts of law, therefore, but also on the budgetary costs of making those rights exercisable or useful in daily life. The public costs of police and fire departments contribute essentially to the "protective perimeter" that makes it possible to enjoy and exercise our basic constitutional and other rights.[6]

DEFINING COSTS

American law draws an important distinction between a "tax" and a "fee." Taxes are levied on the community as a whole, regardless of who captures the benefits of the public services funded thereby. Fees, by contrast, are charged to specific beneficiaries in proportion to the services they personally receive. The individual rights of Americans, including the right to private property, are generally funded by taxes, not by fees.[7] This all-important funding formula signals that, under American law, individual rights are public not private goods.

Admittedly, the quality and extent of rights protection depends on private expenditures as well as on public outlays. Because rights impose costs on private parties as well as on the public budget, they are necessarily worth more to some people than to others. The right to choose one's own defense lawyer is certainly worth more to a wealthy individual than to a poor one. Freedom of the press is more valuable to someone who can afford to purchase dozens of news organizations than to someone who sleeps under one newspaper at a time. Those who can afford to litigate obtain more value from their rights than those who cannot.

But the dependency of rights protection on private resources is well understood and has traditionally attracted greater attention than the dependency of rights protection on *public* resources. Lawyers who work for the American Civil Liberties Union (ACLU) voluntarily accept a cut in personal income in order to defend what they see as fundamental rights. That is a private cost. But the ACLU is also a tax-exempt organization, which means that its activities are partly financed by the public.[8] And this, as we shall see, is only the most trivial way in which rights protection is funded by the ordinary taxpayer.

Rights have social costs as well as budgetary costs. For instance, the harms to private individuals that are sometimes inflicted by criminal suspects released on their own recognizance can reasonably be classed among the social costs of a system that takes serious measures to protect the rights of the accused. A comprehensive study of the costs of rights, therefore, would necessarily devote considerable attention to such nonmonetary costs. But the budgetary costs of rights, treated in isolation from both social costs and private costs, provides an ample and important domain for exploration and analysis. Focusing exclusively on the budget is also the simplest way to draw attention to the fundamental dependence of individual freedoms on collective contributions managed by public officials.

Unlike social costs, "net costs" (and benefits) cannot be temporarily put to one side. Some rights, although costly up front, increase taxable social wealth to such an extent that they can reasonably be considered self-financing. The right to private property is an obvious example. The right to education is another. Even protecting women from domestic violence may be viewed in this way, if it helps bring once-battered wives back into the productive workforce. Public investment in the protection of such rights helps swell the tax base upon which active rights protection, in other areas as well, depends. Obviously enough, the value of a right cannot be assessed by looking solely at its positive contribution to the gross national product (GNP). (While the right of prisoners to minimal medical care is not self-financing, it is no less obligatory than freedom of contract.) But the long-term budgetary impact of expenditures on rights cannot be left out of the picture.

Rights, it should also be noted, may impose a burden on the public fisc beyond their direct costs. A foreign example will help drive this point home. Freedom of movement was created in South Africa by the abolition of the notorious pass laws. But the public costs of building urban infrastructure—water supply, sewage systems, schools, hospitals, and so forth—for the millions who, using their newly won freedom of movement, have flooded from the countryside into cities, is proving astronomically high. (Since the abolition of South Africa's pass laws was one of the most indisputably just acts of recent times, it should not be necessary to prevaricate about its indirect financial costs in order to defend it.) On a more modest scale, here at home, the Third Amendment freedom from having troops quartered in private homes requires that taxpayers fund the construction and maintenance of military barracks. Similarly, a system that scrupulously protects the rights of criminal suspects will make it more costly to apprehend criminals and prevent crimes. And so on.

Such indirect costs or compensatory expenditures, because they directly involve budgetary outlays, fall within the "costs of rights" as narrowly defined in this book. They are especially important because, in some cases, they have led to the curtailment of the rights of Americans. For example, Congress has instructed the secretary of transportation to withhold funding from those states that have not yet abolished the right to ride a motorcycle without a helmet. This decision was based in part on a study made at Congress's request of medical costs associated with motorcycle accidents, including the extent to which private accident insurance fails to cover actual costs. If concern for indirect public costs plays such an important role in the legislative restriction of what some consider our freedoms, the theory of rights obviously cannot leave such costs out.

Finally, this is a book about the nature of legal rights, not a detailed study of public finance. It asks what we can learn about rights by reflecting on their budgetary costs. The rough dollar amounts cited here are therefore meant to be illustrative only. They are certainly not the product of an exhaustive and precise inquiry into the budgetary costs of various rights. To calculate accurately the costs of protecting any given right is immensely complicated, for bookkeeping reasons alone. In 1992, judicial and legal services in the United States cost the taxpayer roughly $21 billion.[9] But joint costs and multi-use facilities make it difficult to specify what portion of this $21 billion was spent on the protection of rights. Similarly, police training presumably improves the humane treatment of suspects and detainees. But while it helps protect their rights, training is primarily intended to increase the capacity of police officers to apprehend criminals and prevent crimes, and in that way to protect the rights of law-abiding citizens. So how could we possibly calculate the exact percentage of the police training budget that is earmarked for the protection of the rights of suspects and detainees?

Empirical research along these lines is certainly desirable. But before such research can be sensibly undertaken, certain conceptual foundations must be laid. To lay such foundations is one of the principal purposes of this book. Once the costs of rights becomes an accepted topic of research, students of public finance will have ample incentive to provide a more precise and thorough account of the dollar amounts devoted to the protection of our basic liberties.

WHY THIS TOPIC HAS BEEN IGNORED

Although the costliness of rights should be a truism, it sounds instead like a paradox, an offense to polite manners, or perhaps even a threat to the preservation of rights. To ascertain that a right has costs is to confess that we have to give something up in order to acquire or secure it. To ignore costs is to leave painful tradeoffs conveniently out of the picture. Disappointed by the way recent conservative majorities on the Supreme Court have limited various rights first granted during the tenure of Chief Justice Earl Warren, liberals may hesitate to throw a spotlight on the public burdens attached to civil liberties. Conservatives, for their part, may prefer to keep quiet about—or, as their rhetoric suggests, may be oblivious to—the way that the taxes of the whole community are used to protect the property rights of wealthy individuals. The widespread desire to portray rights in an unqualifiedly positive light may help explain why a cost-blind approach to the subject has proved congenial to all sides. Indeed, we might even speak here of a cultural taboo—grounded in perhaps realistic worries—against the "costing out" of rights enforcement.

The widespread but obviously mistaken premise that our most fundamental rights are essentially costless cannot be plausibly traced to a failure to detect hidden costs. For one thing, the costs in question are not so terribly hidden. It is self-evident, for instance, that the right to a jury trial entails public costs. A 1989 study provides a dollar amount: the average jury trial in the United States costs the taxpayer roughly $13 thousand.[10] Just as plainly, the right to reasonable compensation for property confiscated under the power of eminent domain has substantial budgetary costs. And the right of appeal in criminal cases clearly assumes that appellate tribunals are publicly funded. And that is not all.

American taxpayers have a serious financial interest in damage suits against local governments involving hundreds of millions of dollars every year in monetary claims. In 1987 alone, New York City paid out $120 million in tort expenses; in 1996, this figure had risen to $282 million.[11] Understandably, every large city in the country is trying to implement tort liability reform, for the right of individuals to sue municipal governments is placing an increasingly intolerable drain on local budgets. Why should judges, narrowly focused on the case before them, have the power to decide that taxpayers' money must be spent on tort remedies rather than, for instance, on schoolbooks or police or child nutrition programs?

Legal professionals understand perfectly well the budgetary implications of the right to sue local governments for damages. They also know that taxpayer money can be saved by openly or surreptitiously curtailing other sorts of rights. The taxpayer's interest in lower taxes can be accommodated, for instance, by defunding defense services for the poor.[12]

Public savings can be achieved just as effectively by tightening standing requirements for civil actions (by curtailing classical rights), as by tightening eligibility requirements for food stamps (by curtailing welfare rights). When judges hold pretrial conferences to encourage out-of-court settlements in order to reduce delay and congestion in court, they implicitly acknowledge that time is money—more specifically, that court time is taxpayers' money. Under the due process clause, government agencies must provide some sort of hearing in connection with taking away a person's liberty or property (including driver's licenses and welfare benefits), but courts routinely take budgetary expenses into account when deciding how elaborate a hearing to hold. In 1976, discussing the procedural safeguards required by a due process guarantee, the Supreme Court said that

> the Government's interest, and hence that of the public, in conserving scarce fiscal and administrative resources is a fac-

tor that must be weighed. At some point the benefit of an additional safeguard to the individual affected by the administrative action and to society, in terms of increased assurance that the action is just, may be outweighed by the cost. Significantly, the cost of protecting those whom the preliminary administrative process has identified as likely to be found undeserving may in the end come out of the pockets of the deserving since resources available for any particular program of social welfare are not unlimited.[13]

Statements of this sort, which have become central to the particular legal question of "how much process is due?" may seem like common sense, but their implications have not yet been fully spelled out or thought through.

In interpreting statutes and precedents, and in deciding who may sue whom, courts of appeal as a matter of course take account of the risk of being overwhelmed by costly suits. More generally, courts are given discretion over their own caseloads because, among other things, public expenditures earmarked for the system of justice are limited. Rules such as the Eleventh Amendment (which bans suits against states for money damages in federal court) suggest that American public officials have always understood the costs to the taxpayer of unrestricted individual rights to sue the government. Today, the nationwide move toward no-fault auto insurance, which restricts the rights of individuals to sue other individuals for personal injury, reflects a growing concern over the exorbitant costs, including public costs, of certain private rights. The rise of medical malpractice tribunals has similar sources. Everyone knows that it is very expensive to make existing facilities readily accessible to people with disabilities as mandated by the Americans with Disabilities Act of 1990. But should it not be just as obvious that taxpayers (who else?) must foot the bill when judges hold that compensation is to be paid for a taking of private property or interpret overcrowding in prison as a violation of the Eighth Amendment prohibition on cruel and unusual punishment?

LIBERALS MAY BE SKEPTICAL INITIALLY about the very subject of this book. But why should cost consciousness diminish our commitment to the protection of basic rights? To ask what rights cost, first of all, is not to ask what they are worth. If we could establish to the last penny what it would cost to enforce, say, the right of equal access to justice in a given budgetary year, we would still not know how much we, as a nation, should spend on it. That is a question for political and moral evaluation, and it cannot be settled by accounting alone.

Such considerations are unlikely to assuage liberal apprehensions, however, given the current and apparently bipartisan crusade to cut public expenditures. Fearing that short-sighted voters may respond all too eagerly to "we cannot afford it" arguments put forward by conservatives, liberals may worry, reasonably enough, that cost-benefit analysis will be misused by powerful private interests. They may fear that inevitable disclosures of waste, inefficiencies, and cost overruns—while good in principle—will eventually lead to a further slashing of budgetary allocations for the protection of even our most precious rights. This fear is not wholly unjustifiable. But its appropriateness depends a good deal on what cost-benefit analysis actually entails.

Conservative anxieties are equally acute, but assume a different hue. Many conservatives cling instinctively to a cost-blind approach to the protection of the so-called negative rights of property and contract, because staring hard at costs would shatter the libertarian fiction that individuals who exercise their rights, in the classic or eighteenth-century sense, are just going about their own business, immaculately independent of the government and the taxpaying community. The public costs of nonwelfare rights show, among other things, that "private wealth," as we know it, exists only because of governmental institutions. Those who attack all welfare programs on principle should be encouraged to contemplate the obvious—namely, that the definition, assignment, interpretation, and protection of property rights is a government service that is delivered to those who currently own property, while being funded out of general revenues extracted from the public at large.

So neither liberals nor conservatives, at the outset, are likely to welcome an inquiry into the costs of rights. And a third obstacle to such a study stems from the distinctive sensibility, and perhaps the vested interests, of the legal profession itself. The judiciary prides itself on being insulated from the political process, following the dictates of reason rather than expediency and commonly deferring to the legislature and executive in fiscal matters. But in practice, judges defer much less in fiscal matters than they appear to, simply because the rights that judges help protect have costs.

That rights are financed by the extractive efforts of the other branches does not mesh smoothly with judicial self-images. The problem is serious. Are judges, though nominally independent, actually dangling on purse strings? Does justice itself hinge on riders attached to spending bills? And how can a judge, given the meager information at his or her disposal (for information too has costs) and his or her immunity to electoral accountability, reasonably and responsibly decide about an optimal allocation of scarce public resources? A judge may compel a street to remain open for expressive activity or a prison to improve living conditions for prisoners, but can that judge be sure that the money he or she commandeers for such ends would not have been used more effectively by inoculating ghetto children against diphtheria?

This dilemma does not affect judges alone. Take civil liberties litigators: because they conceive of rights as weapons with which to confront and attack government, they may be uncomfortable with an inquiry into the budgetary cost of rights that focuses attention on a very simple and concrete way in which rights are "creatures" of government. Generally speaking, the costliness of rights protection explodes a powerful illusion about the relationship between law and politics. If rights depend in practice on the going rate of taxation, then does not the rule of law hinge upon the vagaries of political choice? And is it not demeaning to understand rights, which after all protect human dignity, as grants awarded by the public power (even if the power in question is democratically accountable)? As guardians of priceless values, must not judges, especially, rise above the daily compromises of power-wielders and power-seekers?

Whatever the merits of the "should" in this case, it has little relevance to what "is." To imagine that American law is or can be untouched by the tradeoffs familiar to public finance can only blind us to the political realities of rights protection. For the cost of rights implies, painfully but realistically, that the political branches, which extract and re-allocate public resources, substantially affect the value, scope, and predictability of our rights. If the government does not invest considerable resources to ensure against police abuse, there will be a great deal of police abuse, whatever the law on the books may say. The amount the community chooses to expend decisively affects the extent to which the fundamental rights of Americans are protected and enforced.[14]

ATTENTION TO THE COST OF RIGHTS raises a flurry of additional questions, not just about how much various rights actually cost, but also about who decides how to allocate our scarce public resources for the protection of which rights, and for whom. What principles are commonly invoked to guide these allocations? And can those principles be defended?

Finally, the simple insight that rights have costs points the way toward an appreciation of the inevitability of government and of the various good things that government does, many of which are taken so much for granted that, to the casual observer, they do not appear to involve government at all. Attention to the public costs of individual rights can shed new light upon old questions such as the appropriate dimensions of the regulatory-welfare state and the relationship between modern government and classical liberal rights. Public policy decisions should not be made on the basis of some imaginary hostility between freedom and the tax collector, for if these two were genuinely at odds, all of our basic liberties would be candidates for abolition.

PART I:

WHY A PENNILESS STATE CANNOT PROTECT RIGHTS

Chapter One
ALL RIGHTS ARE POSITIVE

IN *ROE V. WADE*, the Supreme Court ruled that the U.S. Constitution protects a woman's right to have an abortion.[1] A few years later, complications arose: does the Constitution also mandate public funding of abortions? Does it require the government to defray the costs of nontherapeutic abortions if the government is already subsidizing childbirths? In *Maher v. Roe*, the Court concluded that the Constitution does no such thing.[2] A denial of Medicaid payments, it explained, "places no obstacles—absolute or otherwise—in the pregnant woman's path to an abortion." This is because "an indigent woman who desires an abortion suffers no disadvantage as a consequence of the state's decision to fund childbirth," for the government is in no way responsible for her penury. According to the Court, a state legislature's refusal to foot this particular bill, while it may effectively deny safe abortion to a penniless woman, in no way violates that woman's "right" to choose.

To reconcile its holding in *Roe* with that in *Maher*, the Court drew a crucial distinction. It said that "there is a basic difference between direct state interference with a protected activity and state encouragement of an alternative." Apparently, the Constitution can, with unimpeachable consistency, first prohibit the government from intruding and afterward permit the government to withhold support. A woman is constitutionally protected from impermissible restrictions by state agencies, the Court went on to explain. But her freedom of choice does not carry with it "a constitutional entitlement to the financial resources to avail herself of the full range of protected choices." Protection from a burden is one thing, entitlement to a benefit is another. And indeed such a distinction between a liberty and a subsidy sounds like common sense. But is it supportable? On what grounds?

Behind the distinction adduced by the Court lies an unspoken premise: immunity from invasion by the state involves no significant entitlement to financial resources. Theorists who share this assumption see constitutional rights as shields established solely to protect vulnerable individuals from arbitrary imprisonment, intrusions on contractual freedom, takings of property, and other forms of governmental abuse. Personal liberty can be secured, they typically argue, simply by limiting the government's interference with freedom of action and association. Individual freedom requires not governmental performance but only governmental forbearance. Construed along these lines, rights resemble "walls against the state," embodying the assurance that Congress "shall make no laws" restricting private liberty or imposing excessive burdens. By dividing government against itself, the Constitution prevents public authorities from intruding or abridging or infringing. The limited government that results leaves plenty of room for private individuals to mind their own business, to breathe and act freely in unregulated social realms. Such immunity from government meddling is even said to be the essence of constitutionalism. And while action is costly, inaction is relatively cheap, or perhaps free. How could anyone confuse the right to noninterference by public authorities with monetary claims upon the public treasury?

THE FUTILITY OF DICHOTOMY

The opposition between two fundamentally different sorts of claim—between "negative rights" such as those granted in *Roe* and "positive rights" such as those denied in *Maher*—is quite familiar.[3] But it is anything but self-evident. It does not appear anywhere in the Constitution, for one thing. It was wholly unknown to the American framers. So how does it arise? It has profoundly shaped the legal landscape of the United States, but does it provide a cogent classification of different kinds of rights? Does it make sense?

Without some simplifying scheme, admittedly, the plethora of rights entrenched in American law are hard to think about in an orderly fashion. U.S. citizens successfully claim such a cornucopia of rights, and these rights are so palpably diverse, that generalization about them sometimes seems beyond our reach. How should we think systematically about rights so disparate as the right to strike and freedom of conscience, the right to sue journalists for libel and the right to be free from unreasonable searches and seizures? And how should the right to vote be compared to the right to bequeath one's property, or the right of self-defense to freedom of the press? What do these highly variegated claims have in common? And how can we classify or subdivide, in a rational way, the rights protected and enforced in the United States today?

Even a selective list of the everyday rights of ordinary Americans will make our embarrassment of riches clear. It is not easy to arrange in useful categories such strikingly diverse claims as the right to an abortion, the right to practice one's profession, the right to terminate an agreement, the right to be considered

for parole, consumer rights, parental rights, the right to submit evidence before a review board, the right to testify in court,
and the right against self-incrimination. Under what basic
headings should we classify the right to change one's name, the
right of private security guards to make arrests, the exclusive
right to decide who publishes (copyright), stock-purchase
rights, the right to recover money damages for defamation, ten-
ants' and landlords' rights, the right to smoke the dried leaves
of some (but not all) plants, and the right to judicial review of
the rulings of administrative agencies? Are there purposes for
which it is helpful to sort into two basic groupings—say, the
positive and the negative—the right of legislative initiative, the
right not to be denied a job because of sexual preference, the
right to return to a job after taking unpaid maternity leave,
the right to interstate travel, freedom of testation, and the right
to inform authorities of a violation of the law? And what about
hunting and fishing rights, the right to keep and bear arms, a
landowner's right to abate nuisances upon his land, mineral
rights, the right to present testimony about the victim of a
crime in order to influence the sentencing of a perpetrator, pen-
sion rights, the right to give to charity tax-free, the right to
recover a debt, the right to run for office, the right to use extra-
judicial arbitration methods, and the right to view obscene
materials at home? And how should we classify visitation rights
in prison, the right to dispose of one's property as one wishes,
the right of an expelled high school student to a hearing, the
right to marry and divorce, the right of first refusal, the right
to be reimbursed for overpayments, the right to the presence
and advice of an attorney before custodial interrogation by law
enforcement authorities, the right to emigrate, the right to

receive counseling about birth control, and the right to use con-
traceptives?

This ramshackle inventory of only some of the everyday
rights of ordinary Americans suggests the magnitude of the
challenge facing anyone who wants to map the sprawling terrain
of our individual liberties. Even if we set aside archaic-sound-
ing anomalies, such as the "right of rebellion," we will have a
tough time organizing into two mutually exclusive and jointly
exhaustive groups the swarm of claims and counterclaims that
help structure the commonplace expectations and routine
behavior of U.S. citizens today.

THE LURE OF DICHOTOMY

True, grand efforts at simplification cannot be impeded. For
some purposes, moreover, simplification can be useful; the question is whether the relevant simplification helps illuminate reality.[4] Among recent attempts to impose an easily grasped order
on the multiplicity of basic rights invoked and enforced in this
country, the one to which the Supreme Court, for good or ill, has
lent the weight of its authority has been far and away the most
influential. In classrooms and on editorial pages, in judicial
opinions and before congressional committees, a distinction is
routinely drawn between negative rights and positive rights, or
(what is often perceived to be the same thing) between liberties
and subsidies. The distinction gains its initial plausibility, perhaps, because it seems to track the politically more familiar
contrast between small government and big government.

This dichotomy has taken deep root in common thought
and expression. Those Americans who wish to be left alone prize
their immunities from public interference, it is said, while those

who wish to be taken care of seek entitlements to public aid. Negative rights ban and exclude government; positive ones invite and demand government. The former require the hobbling of public officials, while the latter require their affirmative intervention. Negative rights typically protect liberty; positive rights typically promote equality. The former shield a private realm, whereas the latter reallocate tax dollars. The former are privative or obstructionist, while the latter are charitable and contributory. If negative rights shelter us from the government, then positive rights grant us services by the government. The former rights include the rights of property and contract and, of course, freedom from being tortured by the police; the latter encompass rights to food stamps, subsidized housing, and minimal welfare payments.

This storybook distinction between immunities and entitlements has become so influential, even authoritative, that the Supreme Court was able to assume its validity without serious examination or even argument. Neither its relative historical novelty nor its palpable inadequacy has weakened its hold on academic analysis or the public imagination. But wherein lies its seemingly irresistible appeal?

The attraction of this categorization stems partly from the moral warning or moral promise it is believed to convey. Conservative devotees of the positive/negative rights distinction routinely urge, for instance, that welfare rights are potentially infantilizing and exercised on the basis of resources forked out free of charge by the government. Classical liberal rights, they add by way of contrast, are exercised autonomously, American-style, by hardy and self-sufficient individuals who spurn paternalism and government handouts.

Critics of the regulatory-welfare state also interpret the immunities/entitlements dichotomy in the light of a simplified narrative of historical betrayal or decline. Negative rights, they say, were the first liberties to be established, having been wisely institutionalized at the Founding, if not earlier, whereas positive rights were added afterward, in an ill-considered twentieth-century deviation from the original understanding. When the United States was first created, the protection and enforcement of basic rights was limited to guarantees against tyrannical and corrupt government. Only much later—with the New Deal, the Great Society, and the Warren Court—were supererogatory entitlements to public assistance introduced. Instead of protecting us from government, this conservative story continues, welfare rights make people dependent on government, thus eroding "real freedom" in two different ways: by unfairly confiscating the private assets of the wealthy and imprudently weakening the self-sufficiency of the poor. By profligately adding new positive rights to old negative ones, modern liberals such as Franklin Delano Roosevelt and Lyndon Johnson not only betrayed the Founders' conception of freedom, but also summoned into existence a whole flock of impoverished and dependent citizens who now, alas, must be elbowed off the government soup wagon.

This narrative of decline is recounted with palpable earnestness by political conservatives. American progressives could not disagree more. Nevertheless, they too frequently assume that there are basically two kinds of rights, the positive and the negative. They merely redescribe the shift from immunities to entitlements as a progressive tale of evolutionary improvement and moral growth.[5] While conservatives deplore the emergence of taxpayer-subsidized welfare rights, progressives applaud the rise of positive guarantees—interpreting this as a sign of political learning and an improved understanding of the requirements of justice. Charitable impulses have finally come to the fore and been codified into law. New Deal and Great Society America broke with the narrow principles that served the interests of property holders and big business to the detriment of the majority. Viewed with hindsight, negative rights were limited or perhaps even cruel. The eventual rise of positive rights registered a novel appreciation of the need to supplement non-interference with public provision.

One and the same distinction, in effect, obligingly serves two contrary outlooks. While American liberals typically associate rights of property and contract with immoral egoism, American conservatives link private liberties to moral autonomy. Progressives trace entitlements to generous solidarity, while libertarian conservatives connect welfare handouts to sickly dependency. Opposite evaluations are attached, but the conceptual skeleton is the same. Although politically nonpartisan, the negative/positive rights dichotomy is by no means politically innocent, shaping as it does some of our most important debates. It provides the theoretical underpinnings for both attacks on and defenses of the regulatory-welfare state. The negative/positive polarity, we might even say, furnishes a common language within which welfare-state liberals and libertarian conservatives can understand each other and trade abuse.

But who is correct? Are property rights instruments of selfish egoism or sources of personal autonomy? Do welfare rights (including those to medical care or employment training) express solidarity and fellow-feeling or erode initiative and inculcate dependency? Should individuals be protected only from government or also by government? These questions encapsulate much of the American rights debate today. Naturally, any dichotomy that appeals simultaneously to both the Left and the Right is likely to be hard to criticize and immensely difficult to slough off. Taken-for-grantedness, however, does not mean that the distinction is justifiable either descriptively or normatively. Upon inspection, the contrast between two fundamental sorts of rights is more elusive than we might have expected, and much less clear and simple than our Supreme Court has assumed. In fact, it turns out to be based on fundamental confusions, both theoretical and empirical. But if the distinction itself is flawed, then perhaps neither side of the American rights debate is on solid ground.

THE COST OF REMEDIES

"Where there is a right, there is a remedy" is a classical legal maxim. Individuals enjoy rights, in a legal as opposed to a moral sense, only if the wrongs they suffer are fairly and predictably redressed by their government. This simple point goes a long way toward disclosing the inadequacy of the negative rights/positive rights distinction. What it shows is that all legally enforced rights are necessarily positive rights.

Rights are costly because remedies are costly. Enforcement is expensive, especially uniform and fair enforcement; and legal rights are hollow to the extent that they remain unenforced. Formulated differently, almost every right implies a correlative duty, and duties are taken seriously only when dereliction is punished by the public power drawing on the public purse. There are no legally enforceable rights in the absence of legally enforceable duties, which is why law can be permissive only by being simultaneously obligatory. That is to say, personal liberty cannot be secured merely by limiting government interference with freedom of action and association. No right is simply a right to be left alone by public officials. All rights are claims to an affirmative governmental response. All rights, descriptively speaking, amount to entitlements defined and safeguarded by law. A cease-and-desist order handed down by a judge whose injunctions are regularly obeyed is a good example of government "intrusion" for the sake of individual liberty. But government is involved at an even more fundamental level when legislatures and courts define the rights that such judges protect. Every thou-shalt-not, to whomever it is addressed, implies both an affirmative grant of right by the state and a legitimate request for assistance addressed to an agent of the state.

If rights were merely immunities from public interference, the highest virtue of government (so far as the exercise of rights was concerned) would be paralysis or disability. But a disabled state cannot protect personal liberties, even those that seem wholly "negative," such as the right against being tortured by police officers and prison guards. A state that cannot arrange prompt visits to jails and prisons by taxpayer-salaried doctors, prepared to submit credible evidence at trial, cannot effectively protect the incarcerated against tortures and beatings. All rights are costly because all rights presuppose taxpayer funding of effective supervisory machinery for monitoring and enforcement.

The most familiar government monitors of wrongs and enforcers of rights are the courts themselves. Indeed, the notion that rights are basically "walls against the state" often rests upon the confused belief that the judiciary is not a branch of government at all, that judges (who exercise jurisdiction over police-officers, executive agencies, legislatures, and other judges) are not civil servants living off government salaries. But American courts are "ordained and established" by government; they are part and parcel of the state. Judicial accessibility and openness to appeal are crowning achievements of liberal state-building. And their operating expenses are paid by tax revenues funneled successfully to the court and its officers; the judiciary on its own is helpless to extract those revenues. Federal judges in the United States have lifetime tenure, and they are quite free from the supervisory authority of the public prosecutor. But no well-functioning judiciary is financially independent. No court system can operate in a budgetary vacuum. No court can function without receiving regular injections of taxpayers' dollars to finance its efforts to discipline public or private violators of rights, and when those dollars are not forthcoming, rights cannot be vindicated. To the extent that rights enforcement depends upon judicial vigilance, rights cost, at a minimum, whatever it costs to recruit, train, supply, pay, and (in turn) monitor the judicial custodians of our basic rights.

When the holder of a legal right is wronged, he may usually petition a taxpayer-salaried judge for relief. To obtain a remedy, which is a form of government action, the wronged party exercises his right to use the publicly financed system of litigation, which must be kept readily available for this purpose. To have a right, it has been said, is always to be a potential plaintiff or appellant.[6] Rights can be retrenched, as a consequence, by making it harder for complainants to seek vindication before a judge. One way to do this is to deprive courts of their operating funds. To claim a right successfully, by contrast, is to set in motion the coercive and corrective machinery of public authority. This machinery is expensive to operate, and the taxpayer must defray the costs. That is one of the senses in which even apparently negative rights are, in actuality, state-provided benefits.

To protect rights, judges exact obedience. Courts issue injunctions to restrain the unlawful infringement of patents or to force realty companies to rent to African Americans under the Fair Housing Act of 1968. To insure freedom of information, courts order federal agencies to provide information requested by the public. Liberty, in such cases, hinges upon authority. When judicial oversight is lax, rights are correspondingly flimsy or elusive. American immigration authorities routinely discriminate on the basis of physical disability, political opinion, and national origin. To remark that aliens trying to enter the United States have few legal rights is to observe that, under American law, they have little access to publicly funded judicial remedies.

But courts are not the only tax-funded government bodies to deliver remedies. For instance, consumer protection bureaus in various states regularly receive complaints and act to protect consumers' rights by penalizing the unfair and deceptive practices of retailers. At the federal level, the Consumer Product Safety Commission spent $41 million in 1996 identifying and analyzing hazardous products and enforcing manufacturer compliance with federal standards.[7] Many other government agencies serve similar rights-enforcing functions. The Department of Justice itself spent $64 million on "civil rights matters" in 1996. The National Labor Relations Board (NLRB), which cost the taxpayer $170 million in 1996, protects the rights of workers by imposing obligations on management. The Occupational Safety and Health Administration (OSHA)—$306 million expended in 1996—defends the rights of workers by obliging employers to provide a safe and healthy workplace. The Equal Employment Opportunity Commission (EEOC), with a 1996 budget of $233 million, safeguards the rights of employees and job seekers by obliging employers not to discriminate in hiring, firing, promotion, and transfers.[8] In every one of these cases, the cost of enforcing rights can be chalked up to the price of enforcing their correlative duties.

To be sure, it is possible to complain that several or all of these agencies are wasteful or too expensive, or even that some of them should be abolished. But while no particular set of institutions is ideal, some substantial governmental machinery for providing remedies must remain, for rights have nothing to do with autonomy from public authority. Because the wholly private and self-sufficient individual has no rights, it is implausible to be "for rights" and "against government."

A few more examples will help clarify this point. The right to bequeath one's private property to heirs of one's choice— "the right to speak after death"—is obviously a power that no individual testator can exercise autonomously, without the active assistance of state agencies. (Proceedings for construing and establishing the validity of wills, and arbitrating the disputes to which wills sometimes give rise, are managed by probate courts, which are funded by taxpayers, not merely by user fees.) And the right to make an enforceable will is perfectly typical, for *no* rightsholder is autonomous. What would the right to marry mean without public institutions, which must spend taxpayers' money to define and create the institution of marriage? What would the right to child support mean in practice if state agencies could not successfully fulfill requests to locate parents or deduct unpaid support from federal and state tax refunds? What would the copyrights owned by private American entertainment industries be worth in, say, China, if the U.S. government did not put its official weight behind their enforcement?

Something similar can be said about the right to private property. American law protects the property rights of owners not by leaving them alone but by coercively excluding nonowners (say, the homeless) who might otherwise be sorely tempted to trespass. Every creditor has a right to demand that the debtor repay his debt; in practice, this means that the creditor can instigate a two-party judicial procedure against a defaulting debtor in which a delict is ascertained and a sanction imposed. And he can also count on the sheriff to "levy upon" the personal property of the debtor, to sell it, and then to pay the delinquent's debts from the proceeds. The property rights of creditors, like the property rights of landowners, would be empty words without such positive actions by publicly salaried officials.

The financing of basic rights through tax revenues helps us see clearly that rights are public goods: taxpayer-funded and government-managed social services designed to improve collective and individual well-being. All rights are positive rights.

Chapter Two
THE NECESSITY OF
GOVERNMENT PERFORMANCE

THE IDEA THAT RIGHTS ARE ESSENTIALLY AIMED "against" government, rather than calling on government, is patently wrong when applied to what is sometimes called "private law." Rights in contract law and tort law are not only enforced but also created, interpreted, and revised by public agencies. At both federal and state levels, courts and legislatures are constantly creating and readjusting the legal rules that give meaning to rights, as well as specifying and respecifying the various exceptions to these rules. By adjudication and legislation, public authorities not only enforce contracts but also decide which contracts are enforceable and which are unenforceable, unconscionable, or otherwise meaningless pieces of paper. Judges and legislators not only award damages to the victims of negligence but also identify which excuses are legally acceptable for what might otherwise be classified as negligent behavior. The right of American citizens to sue an FBI agent for violating their rights under color of law is wholly defined by statutes and statutory and constitutional interpretation. The rights of out-of-state recreational and commercial fishers owe much of their content to judicial interpretation of the privileges and immunities clause and all of their content to positive law.

The rules defining ordinary rights of this sort are intricate, technical, and full of highly subtle qualifications. In American jurisdictions, for instance, contract law generally stipulates that an injured party cannot collect damages for a loss that he could have avoided after he learned of the breach of contract. An individual who asserts his rights under contract law or tort law must therefore master, or submit to, a complex tissue of rules and exceptions that are, in turn, administered by state officials. He must avail himself of the public power first for the specification of these rules (and exceptions), then for their interpretation, and finally for their enforcement.

The plaintiff's right to bring an action at law against a defendant is not adequately described as a right "against" the state. It is neither a right to be independent of the state nor a right that protects the rightsholder from the state, but rather a right to use state power to give legal effect to a private agreement, to enjoin trespassers from entering private property, to collect compensatory or punitive damages from someone who has negligently or recklessly caused an injury, and so forth. When I sue someone under contract or tort law, I am not trying to get the government "off my back"; I am trying to get it "on my case." In private law, the rightsholder does not need government forbearance; he needs government performance.

To draw attention to the positive role of government in the protection of each and every American liberty is not to deny that, for very limited purposes, some versions of the negative/positive dichotomy may be usefully applied to the analysis of rights. It is perfectly plausible to distinguish between performances and forbearances. The landowner has a legal right that passersby refrain from trespassing on his land. A contract holder may have a right to ensure that third parties do not interfere with an ongoing contractual relationship. In each case, to have a right is to have a legal power to prevent others from acting in a harmful way.[1] Such a right to the self-restraint of others can be usefully contrasted to rights to compel the desirable actions of others, such as the right of a creditor legally to coerce a debtor to repay a debt, or a right of a contracting party to compel his contractual partner to perform.

Because American law recognizes wrongful omissions as well as wrongful commissions, the distinction between rights to require action and rights to prohibit action is useful and important. But it should not be confused with the much less plausible distinction between negative and positive rights, as these concepts are commonly deployed, not only by the Supreme Court. The wholly reasonable distinction between forbearance and performance lends no credence to the opposition between immunity against government interference and entitlement to government service. For the forbearance/performance dichotomy, as just described, does not, in the first instance, refer to government action at all. One private individual has a right either to force another private individual to act or to preclude another private individual from acting. In both cases, obviously, enforcement of a right requires decisive government performance. To protect myself from trespassers and to collect from a delinquent debtor, I have a right to set in motion a tax-funded system of litigation, devoted to accurate fact-finding (which is far from easy) and operated by government bodies—namely, the courts.

How Exceptional Are Constitutional Rights?

But are not private-law rights (such as the right to sue for breach of contract) quite unlike constitutional rights (such as freedom of speech)? It makes little sense to distinguish between property rights and welfare rights by calling the former negative and the latter positive. Is it more plausible to label private-law rights as positive (requiring government action), and constitutional rights as negative (requiring governmental self-restraint)? When speaking of rights against state action, after all, the Supreme Court was referring exclusively to constitutional rights. So this question arises: are the liberties protected under the Bill of Rights wholly negative? Do they require the state to refrain from acting without requiring the state to act?

Some constitutional rights depend for their existence on positive acts by the state, and the government is therefore under a constitutional duty to perform, not to forbear, under the Constitution as it stands. If it allows one person to enslave another, by doing nothing to disrupt an arrangement that amounts to involuntary servitude, the state has violated the Thirteenth Amendment. Under the First Amendment's protection of freedom of speech, states must keep streets and parks open for expressive activity, even though it is expensive to do this, and to do it requires an affirmative act. Under the protection against "takings" of private property without just compensation, the government is probably under an obligation to create trespass law and to make it available to property owners, and a partial or complete repeal of the law of trespass—a failure to act, in other words, to protect private property—would likely be unconstitutional. If a judge accepts a bribe offered by a defendant and therefore does nothing to protect the plaintiff's rights, the judge has violated the due process clause. If a state declines to make its courts available to enforce certain contract rights, it has probably impaired the obligations of contracts, in violation of the contracts clause. In all these cases, the government is obliged, by the Constitution, to protect and to perform.

Practically speaking, the government "enfranchises" citizens by providing the legal facilities, such as polling stations, without which they could not exercise their rights. The right to vote is meaningless if polling place officials fail to show up for work. The right to just compensation for confiscated property is a mockery if the Treasury fails to disburse. The First Amendment right to petition for a redress of grievances is a right of access to government institutions and a right, incidentally, that assumes that the government can perform for the benefit of aggrieved citizens. Nor is this all.

If an agency of the American government tries to deprive anyone of life, liberty, or property, it is required to give that person timely notice and provide an opportunity to be heard before an impartial body. The right to subpoena witnesses in one's own defense is useless if the court's solemn writs and summonses are greeted with laughter. And what does it mean to say that state and federal governments are prohibited from denying equal protection before the law if not that they are required to provide it? Protection against unequal treatment by government officials requires other government officials to receive and resolve complaints. The constitutional right to due process—like the private right to bring an action in contract or tort—presupposes that, at the taxpayers' expense, the state maintains and makes accessible complex and relatively transparent legal institutions within which the cumbersome formalities of fair, public, and understandable adjudication occur.

Admittedly, some important constitutional rights are plausibly styled as duties of the government to forbear rather than to perform. But even those "negative rights"—such as prohibitions on double jeopardy and excessive fines—will be protected only if they find a protector, only if there exists a supervisory state body, usually a court of some kind, able to force its will upon the violators or potential violators of the rights at issue. Even rights reasonably described as operating "against" the state require the (affirmative) creation and strengthening of relations of oversight, command, and obedience so that rogue officials (including police officers and prison guards) do not behave cruelly or discriminatorily. In some cases, public officials must indeed be kept out of protected zones. But those zones qualify as protected only because of affirmative government, and to achieve the desired protection, vulnerable individuals must have relatively easy access to a second, higher-level set of government actors whose decisions are deemed authoritative.

Nonperforming public officials—whether apathetic or bribe-taking or remissly supervised—will not enforce constitutional rights any more effectively than they enforce rights held under statutes and common law. The very idea that a certain kind of process is "due" demonstrates that constitutional rights impose affirmative obligations on the state. Giving citizens access to courts and other adjudicative forums is not like giving them access to natural harbors and navigable waters, because the government must not only brush aside hindrances to access, but must actually create the institutions to which access is being granted. "Avenues of relief" are maintained in passable condition by government officials. The operating expenses of American courts alone run in the billions of dollars every year, and the American taxpayer picks up the tab.

Rights and Powers

Invariably, rights pit power against power. Under tort law, rights enlist the power of government to extract compensatory or punitive damages from private wrongdoers. Under constitutional law, rights bring the power of one branch of government to bear upon wrongdoers from other government agencies. For instance, in the late 1960s, the Supreme Court protected the right of students to wear black armbands to school (in a protest against the Vietnam War) by overruling public high school authorities.[2] Protection "against" government is therefore unthinkable without protection "by" government. This is exactly what Montesquieu had in mind when he asserted that freedom can be protected only if power checks power.[3] No legal system can defend people against public officials without defending people by means of public officials.

When a right is enforced, moreover, somebody wins and somebody loses. The enforcement of a right (whether it is a right against racial discrimination or a right to collect compensatory damages) is "accepted" by the losing party because that party has no choice, that is, because the full power of the state has come down on the side of the rightsholder, and thus against the losing party. Conversely, curtailing a right often involves curtailing the power of the government agency that enforces it in the face of serious resistance. For instance, if a political pressure group wants to cut back the existing rights of American workers, it will try to diminish the authority of OSHA, the EEOC, or the NLRB. This is strong evidence that rights depend essentially on power.

The dependency of liberty on authority should be especially

obvious in the United States, where rights against abuse by state and local officials have long been enforced by federal officials. The "incorporation doctrine," which extends most of the Bill of Rights to the states, protects individual liberties not by removing government from the scene, but by giving national authorities the power to overrule state authorities. The Fourteenth Amendment prohibits the states from denying anyone equal protection of the law or depriving them of life, liberty, or property without due process of law. Such a prohibition would be hollow if the federal government did not have the power to bear down on recalcitrant states.

"Congress shall have power to enforce this article by appropriate legislation." All three Civil War amendments contain such enforcement clauses. So the amended Constitution explicitly vests the federal government with the capacity to realize in practice the individual rights it proclaims in principle. Without such governmental powers, rights would have no "bite." To protect the rights of southern blacks, more than once in our history the national government has dispatched federal troops to the South. Without such a show of force, the individual rights of a large group of Americans would have remained a cruel charade. To prevent racial segregation in education, national involvement was necessary, sometimes including the threat to meet violence with violence. Until Congress and the former Department of Health, Education, and Welfare applied irresistible financial pressure, in any case, school districts in the deep South simply ignored the Supreme Court's desegregation orders. When state government is discriminating, the right to be free from racial discrimination, like the right to property, requires affirmative assistance from government, in this case the nation itself.

In the area of voting rights, the same pattern has prevailed. The Voting Rights Act of 1964—designed to vindicate constitutional rights—called for more involvement by the national government, not less. Until Congress legally prohibited the use of literacy tests, states contrived to disenfranchise black Americans for reasons of race. This is just a further illustration of a general truth: individual rights are invariably an expression of governmental power and authority.

Not included in the original Constitution, the Bill of Rights was added to the Constitution two years after its ratification partly to appease those who desired a weaker and more constrained national government. But that was not its only purpose, and that has not been its effect in practice. By extending the scope of the Bill of Rights, the Supreme Court, a national institution, has steadily encroached on preserves of state power. State autonomy has been whittled away and federal power correspondingly enhanced in the name of individual rights. (Admittedly, the opposite has also occasionally occurred.) Indeed, one of the consequences of the enhancement of federal power has been to apply the prohibition on uncompensated takings of private property to the states—requiring state governments, for instance, to compensate people, as a matter of federal constitutional law, when regulation has rendered their beachfront property valueless.

Decentralizing government has no logical connection with limiting the encroachment of government into society. Many of the original limits on Congress's authority were not meant to preserve immunity from government, but simply to clear a space for unsupervised state regulation, as opposed to federal regulation, of private economic behavior. To create a national market, against the protectionist impulses of local authorities, the federal government had no choice but to erode state regulatory autonomy. And this is perfectly normal: a lower authority will usually retreat only when a higher authority steps forward.

The framers of the American Constitution sought to establish a strong and effective government armed with capacities that the anemic government created under the Articles of Confederation notoriously lacked. A constitution that does not organize effective and publicly supported government, capable of taxing and spending, will necessarily fail to protect rights in practice. This has been a lesson long in learning, and not only for libertarians and free-market economists, but also for some human-rights advocates who have selflessly devoted their careers to a militant campaign against brutal and over-mighty states. All-out adversaries of state power cannot be consistent defenders of individual rights, for rights are an enforced uniformity, imposed by the government and funded by the public. Equal treatment before the law cannot be secured over a vast territory without relatively effective, honest, centralized bureaucratic agencies capable of creating and enforcing rights.

Chapter Three
NO PROPERTY WITHOUT TAXATION

ACCORDING TO THE BRITISH PHILOSOPHER JEREMY BENTHAM, "property and law are born together and die together. Before the laws there was no property; take away the laws, all property ceases."[1] Every first-year law student learns that private property is not an "object" or a "thing" but a complex bundle of rights. Property is a legally constructed social relation, a cluster of legislatively and judicially created and judicially enforceable rules of access and exclusion. Without government, capable of laying down and enforcing compliance with such rules, there would be no right to use, enjoy, destroy, or dispose of the things we own. This is obviously true for rights to intangible property (such as bank accounts, stocks, or trademarks), for the right to such property cannot be asserted by taking physical possession, only by an action at law. But it is equally true of tangible property. If the wielders of the police power are not on your side, you will not successfully "assert your right" to enter your own home and make use of its contents. Property rights are meaningful only if public authorities use coercion to exclude nonowners, who, in the absence of law, might well trespass on property that owners wish to maintain as an inviolable sanctuary. Moreover, to the extent that markets presuppose a reliable system of recordation, protecting title from never-ending challenge, property rights simultaneously presuppose the existence of many competent and honest and adequately paid civil servants outside the police force. My rights to enter, use, exclude from, sell, bequeath, mortgage, and abate nuisances threatening "my" property palpably presuppose a well-organized and well-funded court system.

A liberal government must refrain from violating rights. It must "respect" rights. But this way of speaking is misleading because it reduces the government's role to that of a nonpartici-pant observer. A liberal legal system does not merely protect and defend property. It defines and thus creates property. Without legislation and adjudication there can be no property rights in the way Americans understand that term. Government lays down the rules of ownership specifying who owns what and how particular individuals acquire specific ownership rights. It iden-tifies, for instance, the maintenance and repair obligations of landlords and how jointly owned property is to be sold. It there-fore makes no more sense to associate property rights with "free-dom from government" than to associate the right to play chess with freedom from the rules of chess. Property rights exist because possession and use are created and regulated by law.

Government must obviously help maintain owner control over resources, predictably penalizing force and fraud and other infractions of the rules of the game. Much of the civil law of property and tort is designed to carry out this business. And the criminal justice system channels considerable public resources to the deterrence of crimes against property: larceny, burglary, shoplifting, embezzlement, extortion, the forging of wills, receiving stolen goods, blackmail, arson, and so forth. The criminal law (inflicting punishments) and the civil law (exacting restitution or compensation) conduct a permanent, two-front, and publicly financed war on those who offend against the rights of owners.

David Hume, the Scottish philosopher, liked to point out that private property is a monopoly granted and maintained by public authority at the public's expense. As the English jurist William Blackstone, following Hume, also explained, property is "a political establishment."[2] In drawing attention to the relation between property and law—which is to say, between property and government—Bentham was making the very same point. The private sphere of property relations takes its present form thanks to the political organization of society. Private property depends for its very existence on the quality of public institutions and on state action, including credible threats of prosecution and civil action.

What needs to be added to these observations is the correlative proposition that property rights depend on a state that is willing to tax and spend. Property rights are costly to enforce. To identify the precise monetary sum devoted to the protection of property rights, of course, raises difficult issues of accounting. But this much is clear: a state that could not, under specified conditions, "take" private assets could not protect them effectively, either. The security of acquisitions and transactions depend, in a rudimentary sense, on the government's ability to extract resources from private citizens and apply them to public purposes. On balance, property rights may even place a charge upon the public treasury that vies with the burden of our massive entitlement programs.

None of this denies that protection of property rights can be a valuable investment that increases aggregate wealth over time. On the contrary, the extraction and redistribution of resources necessary to protect property rights is relatively easy to justify. Indeed, American liberalism, like its counterparts elsewhere in the world, is based on the reasonable premise that public investment in the creation and maintenance of a system of private property is richly repaid, not least of all because reliably enforced property rights help increase social wealth and therefore, among other benefits, swell the tax base upon which government can draw to protect other kinds of rights. But the strategic wisdom of an initial investment does not undo the fact that it is an investment.

The immense up-front costs of protecting private property mount even higher if we include, as we surely must, protection from foreign looters and marauders. The thousands of civilians expelled from their homes in Abkhazia or Bosnia—like other forced migrants throughout the world—know that property rights are a mirage without military forces trained and equipped to protect owners from forcible seizures by invading armies or drunken paramilitary gangs. The defense budget in a free-market society is a widely shared public contribution to, among other ends, the protection of private property. Americans spent $265 billion in 1996 on defense and an additional $20 billion on veterans' benefits and services.[3] Military expenditures must unquestionably be counted among the public costs of the property rights that many Americans peaceably exercise and enjoy.

Conscription of low-income youth represents an important way in which property holders may benefit directly from the "civic contributions" of the propertyless. Individual property holders are fundamentally dependent on collective efforts, both diplomatic and military, organized by the government, to protect their land and housing stock from seizure by property-grabbing adjacent states. Montana "Freemen," citizens of the Republic of Texas, and other self-styled government-bashers who pretend they can defend their autonomy with mail-order shotguns and hunting rifles would, in reality, be wholly unable to prevent their private property from being gobbled up even by relatively weak foreign powers if most of their fellow citizens did not regularly submit themselves to taxation and conscription by the national political community.

Where real estate is involved, in fact, ownership becomes quickly enmeshed with sovereignty (or with aspirations to sovereignty, as Palestinians caught selling land to Israelis find out). Defense spending is surely the most dramatic example of the dependency of private rights on public resources. It reveals the statist preconditions of laissez-faire, the authority that underwrites liberty. At common law, only the sovereign is said to have an absolute interest in land: ordinary landowners "hold of the sovereign." This quaint legalism expresses a deep truth. An autonomous individual, in a liberal society, cannot create the conditions of his own autonomy autonomously, but only collectively.

The most ardent antigovernment libertarian tacitly accepts his own dependency on government, even while rhetorically denouncing signs of dependency in others. This double-think is the core of the American libertarian stance. Those who propagate a libertarian philosophy—such as Robert Nozick, Charles Murray, and Richard Epstein—speak fondly of the "minimal state." But describing a political system that is genuinely capable of repressing force and fraud as "minimal" is to suggest, against all historical evidence, that such a system is easy to achieve and maintain. It is not. One piece of evidence to the contrary is the amount we spend, as a nation, to protect private property by punishing and deterring acquisitive crimes. In 1992, for instance, direct expenditures in the United States for police protection and criminal corrections ran to some $73 billion—an amount that exceeds the entire GDP of more than half of the countries in the world.[4] Much of this public expenditure, naturally, was devoted to protecting private property. Even a purportedly hands-off state, if it wants to be serious about encouraging economic activity, must reliably protect homeowners and shopkeepers from burglars, arsonists, and other threats.

An effective liberal government, designed to repress force and fraud, must avoid arbitrary and authoritarian tactics. Those who wield the tools of coercion must be institutionally disciplined into using it for public, not private, purposes. Ideally conceived, a liberal government extracts resources from society fairly and efficiently and redeploys them skillfully and responsibly to produce socially useful public goods and services, such as the deterrence of theft. A successful liberal state must be politically well organized in precisely this sense. Its government must be capable of creating a favorable business climate in which investors are confident that they will reap rewards tomorrow for efforts made today. Without such a state, well-functioning markets, capable of producing prosperity, are very unlikely to emerge or survive. A state capable of reliably repressing force and fraud and enforcing property rights is a cooperative achievement of the first magnitude, and the world is unfortunately filled with negative examples. But if private rights depend essentially on public resources, there can be no fundamental opposition between "government" and "free markets," no contradiction between politically orchestrated social cooperation and footloose individual liberty.

Property owners are far from being self-reliant. They depend on social cooperation orchestrated by government officials. Defense against land-grabbing foreign predators is only one example of the way liberal individualism depends on effective collective action. Recordation is another. American taxpayers expended $203 million for general property and records management in 1997.[5] Sunk costs in our recordation system are much larger. For real estate markets to operate effectively, a reliable system of titles, deeds, and land surveys must be in place. Land registries and offices of public records require skilled and honest staffs. The "free market" is unlikely to put roofs on public buildings where records are stored or establish criminal penalties to deter bribery of officials in charge of registering titles to real or personal property. Surveyors, too, must be paid and monitored. The bare unobstructed latitude to buy and sell private property will not produce an explosion of mutually beneficial private exchanges unless potential buyers receive some sort of guarantee that the putative owner is selling something he (and he alone) actually owns. Without clearly defined, unambiguously assigned, and legally enforceable property rights, ownership does not encourage stewardship. Title holders will neither cultivate their fields nor repair their homes if their rights are not reliably protected by the public power.

Additional examples of government expenditures for the sake of private property owners are legion; it is unnecessary to think that all or even most are defensible in order to see the basic pattern. The American taxpayer spent almost $10 billion in 1996 for agricultural subsidies designed to increase the value of the private property rights of American farmers.[6] The Army Corps of Engineers expended around $1.5 billion in 1996 on flood-plain management and other forms of flood control.[7] The Coast Guard spent $1.26 billion in the same year in search and rescue missions, aids to navigation, marine safety (including the removal of dangerous wrecks and derelicts at sea), ice breaking, and so forth, all of which helps protect the private property of American shippers and boat owners.[8] Copyright, which is a form of property, also involves public expenditure. The Copyright Office and Copyright Royalty Tribunal, taken together, cost $28 million in 1996; $18 million of this amount was covered by user fees, leaving roughly $10 million on the tab of the ordinary taxpayer.[9]

The relatively high rate of owner occupancy in the United States is a creation not only of governmentally conferred rights but also of American mortgage, insurance, and tax law. It is certainly not a product of government disengagement or laissez-faire. Some property owners would be forced to liquidate their holdings if they were not allowed to deduct the depreciation of their assets from their taxable income. And a tax deduction is a form of public subsidy. This is just one more example of the way private property is affirmatively sustained by public subsidies.

Private property is not only protected by government agencies, such as the fire department. It is, more generally, a creation of state action. Legislators and judges define the rules of ownership, just as they establish and interpret the regulations governing all of our basic rights. Does the accidental finder of goods have a legal right to judicial protection? Does a purchaser acquire an ownership right to property bought for value and in good faith from a thief? What rights against a present occupant belong to the owner of a future interest in real property? How many years of wrongful possession destroy the title of the original owner? Can an illegitimate child inherit from its natural parents by intestate succession? What happens if one joint owner sells his portion of jointly owned property? Can I, without notice, cut off branches from my neighbor's tree if they overhang my land? Do I have a right to pile a mountain of garbage in my front yard? Can I build an electrical fence around my land with voltage high enough to kill trespassers? Can I erect a building that cuts off my neighbor's vista? Can I advertise the free viewing of pornographic videos in my front window? Can I stick posters on my neighbor's fence? Under what conditions is copyright assignable? How much do which creditors collect in case of bankruptcy? What rights do pawnbrokers have over goods left to them upon pledge?

Thousands of questions of this sort are continuously asked by those who have property rights and regularly answered by legislatures and courts, that is, by state agencies. The answers given shift over time. In the United States, answers also vary from one jurisdiction to another. For instance, spouses have a right to income from each others' property in Idaho, Louisiana, Texas, and Wisconsin. In most of the rest of the country, they have no such rights. The state cannot "leave the owner alone," therefore, because an owner is an owner only on the precise terms laid down at particular times by specific legislatures and courts.

To protect our property rights, American courts must administer a technically intricate and changing body of rules. These rules are especially vital when two or more individuals have overlapping claims to the same piece of property. Private property as we know it exists only because legislation and adjudication has specified the respective ownership rights of rival claimants—for instance, the property rights of authors and publishers in a book or the property rights of employers and employees in the invention of employees. Upon the death of a co-owner of real property, the law must decide if ownership rights are to be transferred to the living co-owner(s) or to the heirs of the deceased co-owner. The law assigns property rights by creating and enforcing rules for authoritatively settling disputes among rival claimants. To perform this function, judges must be trained, equipped, paid, protected from extortion, and provided with a technical and clerical staff. This is what it means to call the right to property a privately enjoyed public service.

Along the same lines, the basic ingredients of the law of tort—for example, my right to demand compensatory damages from those who have negligently or willfully damaged my property—strongly suggest that property rights are less like latitudes and more like entitlements than American public rhetoric commonly allows. Those who demand greater rights to compensation from government for public "takings"—through regulation or otherwise—are in reality seeking entitlements. They want to be protected publicly and through law. This is not an argument against their claim of right. The regulatory state might well work better if government had to pay property owners for the diminished value of land whenever, for example, new environmental regulations have impeded development. But arguments to this effect should not be based on undiscriminating protests against public invasions of autonomously held rights.

Many political conservatives, but not they alone, urge government to "get out of the marketplace." For their part, some liberals counter that government quite legitimately interferes with, or "steps into," the market whenever and wherever disadvantaged Americans are at risk. But this familiar debate is built on sand. No sharp line can be drawn between markets and government: the two entities have no existence detached from one another. Markets do not create prosperity beyond the "protective perimeter" of the law; they function well only with reliable legislative and judicial assistance.[10]

Of course, inept governments can and do commit economic blunders. Without doubt, ill-devised and poorly timed policies can and do make markets function poorly. The question is not free markets *or* government but what kind of markets and what kind of government. Governments not only have to lay the essential legislative and administrative foundations for a functioning market economy, they can also act to make market systems more productive. They do so, for example, by adjusting the exchange rate of the national tender against foreign currencies, by disrupting anticompetitive monopolies, by building bridges and railroads, and by financing the vocational training of the future workforce. As even Friedrich Hayek, the great critic of socialism, remarked, "The question whether the state should or should not 'act' or 'interfere' poses an altogether false alternative, and the term 'laissez-faire' is a highly ambiguous and misleading description of the principles on which a liberal policy is based."[11]

A liberal economy cannot function unless people are willing to rely on each other's word. For a market to be national, and not merely local, reliance must extend beyond a small circle of mutual acquaintances. In such a system, reliance on the word of relative strangers cannot arise from personal reputations for fairness alone. It must be cultivated and reinforced by public institutions. For one thing, the government must make courts and other institutions available to enforce contracts. Public authorities cultivate the "reliance interest" by attaching property and foreclosing liens. Judges can send an individual to jail for contempt of court if he fails to comply with an order to carry out a contract lawfully entered into. Likewise, laws against defamation, geared to the protection of business and financial reputations, help foster economically beneficial social trust. If contracts were not reliably enforced, it would be more difficult and perhaps even impossible to buy goods on credit or by installment. Without the active help of a sheriff, authorized by a court writ, a seller could not easily repossess consumer goods from a defaulting installment purchaser. More generally, payment by the installment plan, beneficial for the economy as a whole, would be shunned if contracts were not reliably enforced.

In the truly autonomous realm, beyond the reach of government, property is not well protected. (In the abandoned warehouse at the edge of town where you lost your wallet, your right to your property is not worth much.) Where the public power cannot effectively intrude, moreover, extortion is rampant and borrowers are unable to obtain long-term loans, for one function of the liberal state is to lengthen the time horizons of private actors by predictably enforcing known and stable rules. Property is worth little if you, and potential purchasers, do not believe in the future. Confidence in long-term stability is partly a product of reliable law enforcement, that is, of forceful and decisive state action.

But the first thing a government must do to make a market system work is to overcome the age-old rule of force and threats of force. Free markets do not function properly if profit-seekers uninhibitedly engage in criminal violence. Libertarians recognize this fact, but they fail to appreciate the extent to which it undermines their boasted opposition to "government" as well as to taxing and spending. Long-gestation investment in productive facilities, which creates jobs, is unlikely where assets are indefensible against private extortionists. Neoclassical economics supposes that private competitors will not resort to violent crime in the pursuit of gain. Within its own framework, laissez-faire theory is helpless to explain the basis of civilization, the general renunciation of violence by advantage-seeking individuals and groups. Why do most American entrepreneurs hesitate to threaten and kill their competitors? The theory of free markets, as it is currently taught in American universities, tacitly assumes that the problems of short time horizons and violent competition, characterizing the state of nature, have already been solved. For the most part, in other words, the science of economics (unlike, say, the science of anthropology) tacitly presupposes the existence of an active and reliable system of criminal justice.

Even on their own terms, doctrinaire libertarians must acknowledge that government cannot "pull out" of the economy without leaving private individuals helplessly vulnerable to ruthless predators. The relatively peaceful exchange of goods and services, as we know it, is a product of civilized self-restraint and therefore should be understood as a historically improbable and fragile achievement. In the state of nature, a handful of killers and thieves willing to employ deadly force and hazard their lives on a dare can cow a large civilian population. They can establish anticompetitive monopolies, for instance, and dramatically shrink the sphere of voluntary exchange. Only a reliable public power can break such an anarchical reign of fear and legal uncertainty. Only a state can create a vibrant market. Furthermore, only a national government can weave together disconnected local markets into a single national market. For why would a wholesaler in New Jersey sell to a retailer in California if contracts could not be reliably enforced across state lines?

If the government wholly disengages from the economy, the economy will not be free in the sense we admire, and it will certainly not produce the historically unprecedented prosperity to which many Americans have grown accustomed. Voluntary exchanges will occur, as they do even in the poorest of countries, and we may see inchoate versions of well-functioning markets. But government inaction creates an economic system vexed by force, monopoly, intimidation, and narrow localisms. The individual's freedom, his "right to be left alone" by thugs and thieves, cannot be separated from his entitlement to state help—that is, his claim to a range of public services (basic legal provisions and protections) from the government. The effort of social coordination it takes to build even a "minimal" state, capable of repressing force and threats of force, is truly massive and should not be taken for granted.

Capitalists certainly know this and tend not to invest where political risk is excessive, as in some of the emerging Eastern European democracies. Their problem is not too much government but too little government. When government is incoherent, incompetent, and unpredictable, economic actors do not think very far into the future. Not free-enterprise but robber capitalism—the rule of the violent and the unscrupulous—thrives in the absence of law and order.

Swindling is nearly as great a threat to free markets as force, and enforceable antifraud law also presupposes a well-organized and effective system of governance. To some extent markets themselves will deter fraud; people who lie and cheat at the drop of a hat tend not to compete well. But without effective antifraud legislation, private parties will often hesitate to undertake what both sides nevertheless anticipate would be a mutually advantageous voluntary exchange. Antifraud legislation, in turn, costs taxpayer money to enforce. The Federal Trade Commission (FTC) spent $31 million in 1996 investigating unfair and deceptive practices and removing other obstacles to market performance.[12] Perhaps this is too much, perhaps the case for an FTC is weak, but any market requires governmental assistance in protecting against fraud, and that assistance is likely to be costly.

The Securities and Exchange Commission (SEC), through its "full disclosure" program (which cost the taxpayer $58 million in 1996), requires publicly traded companies to furnish management, financial, and business information on a regular basis so that investors will be able to make informed decisions. The SEC spent an additional $101 million in 1996 on the prevention and suppression of fraud in the securities market.[13] Oversight of the stock market and commodity futures market cost the American taxpayer $355 million in 1996.[14]

In the absence of government machinery capable of detecting and remedying misrepresentation and false dealing, free exchange would be an even more risky business than it is. The act of buying and selling is often worrisome in the absence of reliable means to counteract the asymmetry of knowledge between buyer and seller. The seller frequently knows something the buyer needs to know. That is one reason why the risk-averse fear commercial exchanges as possible scams, why they cling to suppliers they know personally rather than shopping around for bargains. Public officials can discourage this kind of clinging, promote market ordering, and discourage swindlers by insuring against any damage arising from the asymmetry of information between buyers and sellers. To help consumers make rational choices about where to obtain credit, for instance, the Consumer Credit Protection Act forces any organization that extends credit to disclose its finance charges and annual percentage rate. Just so, consumers benefit from competitive markets in restaurants because, as voters and taxpayers, they have created and funded sanitation boards that allow them to range adventurously beyond a restricted circle of personally known and trusted establishments. The enforcement of disclosure rules or antifraud statutes is no less a taxpayer-funded spur to market behavior than government inspection of food handlers.

The appropriate level of federal spending and government oversight will remain controversial. Nothing said above is intended as a defense of any particular program; some existing programs should undoubtedly be scaled down. What cannot be denied is that enforceable antifraud legislation is a common good, embodying biblically simple moral principles (keep your promises, tell the truth, cheating is wrong). Moreover, the benefits of antifraud law cannot be captured by a few but are diffused widely throughout society. It is a public service, collectively provided, and serving to reduce transaction costs and promote a free-wheeling atmosphere of buying and selling that would be very unlikely to arise if "caveat emptor!" were the sole rule.

Admittedly, the current economic boom in China suggests that, when suitably integrated into the world economy, a society without a strong court system can use kinship and other informal networks to breed credible commitments even in the absence of reliable judicial enforcement of property rights. In most industrialized societies and as a general rule, however, free markets depend on enforceable contract law and a liberal style of governance. To deter fraud, a government must be interventionist and well funded. American taxpayers have proven willing to foot the bill partly because they see the obvious advantages in the monitoring of private exchanges by politically accountable officials.

Government must not only repress force and fraud, invest in infrastructure and skills, enforce stockholders' rights, and provide securities exchange oversight and patent and trademark protection. It must legally clarify the status of collateral. And it must regulate the banking sector and credit markets to prevent pyramid schemes and ensure a steady flow of credit to businesses rather than cronies. The enforcement of antitrust law is also crucial. For the reliable delivery of these public services, markets require government. At the taxpayer's expense, the state must foster innovation, encourage investment, boost worker productivity, raise production standards, or stimulate the efficient use of scarce resources. It can do this, among other ways, by defining property and contract rights clearly, assigning them unambiguously, and protecting them impartially and reliably. The job is neither easy nor cheap.

To do all this, governments need first to collect money through taxation and then to channel it intelligently and responsibly. Rights enforcement of the sort presupposed by well-functioning markets always involves "taxing and spending." Needless to say, the inevitable dependency of markets on law, bureaucracy, and public policy does not imply that government initiatives are always wise or beneficial. As a political community, we have choices—but only among competing regulatory regimes.

Chapter Four
WATCHDOGS MUST BE PAID

IN 1992, THE ADMINISTRATION OF JUSTICE in the United States—including enforcement, litigation, adjudication, and correction—cost the taxpayer around $94 billion.[1] Included in this allocation were funds earmarked for the protection of the basic rights of suspects and detainees. Because it always presupposes the creation and maintenance of relations of authority, the protection of individual rights is never free. True of the rights of property and contract, this also applies to the rights protected within our system of criminal justice, including of course the rights of people who are not in fact criminals. Here again, rights enforcers must be in a position to tell potential rights violators what to do and what not to do. The history of *habeas corpus* confirms the validity of the thesis that an abusive power can be successfully counterattacked only by another power. Classical liberal rights necessarily depend on relations of command and obedience that, in turn, are expensive to create and maintain. This can be observed clearly in the case of prisoners, whose rights cannot be even minimally protected unless their custodians are monitored from above and penalized for abuses. Although sometimes denounced as a hindrance to law enforcement, protecting the rights of prisoners means nothing more than forcing correctional officers to obey the law. These rights are sometimes controversial, but the basic point—the need to monitor public officials who exercise coercion—is quite general and applies, in different forms, to the rights of the law-abiding as well as of those convicted of crimes.

Protecting prisoners' rights, even quite modestly, is costly. To avoid degrading treatment, prison cells must be ventilated, heated, lit, and cleaned. Prison food must provide minimal nutrition. The Eighth Amendment demands that prison wardens and guards provide minimally humane conditions of confinement. A prison official violates a constitutional right where the deprivation alleged is, objectively, "sufficiently serious"[2] and if he acts with "deliberate indifference" to inmate health and safety. In the federal prison system alone, medical care costs ran to $53 million in 1996.[3] Authorities cannot segregate inmates from the general prison population without using fair procedures. Officials institutionally positioned to penalize flagrant abuses (such as murder or torture) must "monitor the monitors." And to assure access to the appeals process, prison authorities must provide prisoners with "adequate law libraries or adequate assistance to persons trained in the law."[4]

In other words, the right to be treated decently in the system of criminal justice—by police, prosecutors, judges, prison guards, and probation officers—presupposes the power of bureaucratic superiors to punish and deter misconduct by subordinates. Procedures must be established and responsibility assigned for determining the legality or illegality of detention. The enforceable rights of the interrogated are the enforceable duties of the interrogators. The rights of prisoners are the duties of wardens and guards. Protecting rights within the American criminal justice system requires oversight of the law-enforcement apparatus. Whatever their attitude toward red tape, defenders of rights cannot be consistently antibureaucratic, for police and prison guards behave more decently when monitored than when unwatched. And second-level supervisory personnel must be given adequate training and paid a living wage.

The cost of training and monitoring correctional officers is a concrete illustration of the indispensable contribution of the tax-paying community to the protection of individual liberties.[5] True, it is more familiar to style the rights protected within our criminal justice system as purely negative, as rights against the government, as shields from police and prosecutorial and custodial abuse. But attention to the cost of rights should help us focus attention on the other side of the coin, namely on the forms of state action required for rights of suspects and detainees to be a palpable reality rather than a mere paper promise. Nor, it is important to emphasize, are the rights protected by the criminal justice system solely protections of criminals, or even of the wrongly accused. Ordinary citizens depend, for their protection against the state and thus for their so-called negative liberties, on the taxpayer-funded training and monitoring of the police.

Because it involves federal supremacy, the extension of most Fourth, Fifth, and Sixth Amendment protections to individuals suspected, accused, or convicted of crimes within the states nicely exemplifies the positive side of ostensibly negative rights. The government, as the agent of American taxpayers, provides the accused with certain weapons (rights) which, it is expected or hoped, will help reduce improper conduct by officials and even the odds against the occasionally overwhelming power of the prosecution. Thus, the right to a speedy, fair, and public jury trial is an entitlement to a taxpayer-funded benefit or service.

Needless to say, the rights of accused Americans—rich and poor, black and white—are not protected equally. But our criminal justice system would be even more grossly unfair if the community as a whole did not subsidize some basic protections. In the 1996 U.S. budget, covering only federal trials, $81 million went to fees and expenses for obtaining witnesses.[6] The accused does not have to rely on his own resources to compel witnesses to testify in his favor; he is legally entitled to employ resources drawn from the community as a whole. Ability to pay bears no rational relation to innocence or guilt. This, at least, is the Supreme Court's explicit rationale for the right of the indigent accused, even on appeal, to a lawyer whose salary will be paid by the public. Equal protection implies a constitutional right of access to whatever appellate process a state makes generally available.[7] Under existing law, American taxpayers must pay for blood grouping tests for indigent defendants in paternity cases and for psychiatric assistance for indigent defendants in some criminal cases. And to ensure that court-appointed attorneys are not in the pocket of the prosecutor, some sort of independent supervision is obviously required.

Even the right of the accused to be free pending trial presupposes the bureaucratic capacity to set up and administer systems of bail and release on recognizance. Such a right would be unavailable if the state could not perform—that is, if the criminal justice system could not, with relative accuracy, distinguish defendants who will show up for trial from those likely to jump bail, or train its police well enough to conduct a competent investigation without keeping suspects uninterruptedly behind bars.

The duty of the police to refrain from unreasonable searches and seizures is meaningless unless the courts have the capacity to compel the police to comply with the Constitution. This capacity depends importantly on social norms and expectations and on the training and norms of the police, but it also depends on the fiscal wherewithal of the judiciary. Searches must be authorized in advance by warrants issued by neutral and detached magistrates upon proof of probable cause, and the salaries of these nonpartisan judges cannot be manipulated in an ad hoc manner by officials in the other branches of government. The exclusionary rule, barring from trial any evidence gathered illegally, is one way the American judiciary has tried to enforce police compliance or at least to offer constitutional instructions to officers engaged in crime prevention. The exclusionary rule has been gradually softened by exceptions, to be sure. But why has this tendency to diminish the pre-existing rights of suspects and defendants been supported by those who want to be tough on crime? Only because such a rule represents a form of supervisory interference thought to handcuff the police and weaken the fight against crime by permitting police illegality to taint otherwise solid evidence. To erode a right—whether desirable or not—often means impairing a publicly funded supervisory power.

In effect, the rights of the accused and the incarcerated contract and expand as the American judiciary is sometimes more, sometimes less deferential toward the executive branch's war on crime. This oscillation shows, yet again, that the breadth of our liberties depends upon the resolve of our authorities. But it is worth stressing that rights cannot be based on government forbearance, for an even more basic reason. Rights come into being only after a government agency, often a court, makes the effort to define such basic terms as "excessive," "reasonable," and "cruel." The precise scope of our rights changes over time as the courts decide. The court's job is not simply to prevent the executive branch from acting abusively (taking that term as a rough placeholder for what the Constitution forbids). It also has to set down the criteria for distinguishing abusive from nonabusive action. This is an affirmative task it cannot avoid. When is a search or seizure unreasonable? At what point in time does a suspect have a right to counsel—already at the line-up, or only at the preliminary hearing? Under what conditions can officers initiate interrogation? In the criminal justice system, rights always presuppose at least one form of state action because they always assume that the court has given answers, for better or worse, to these and other similar questions. Judicial inaction, a refusal to answer, is not an option.

The Rehnquist Court has reinterpreted and thus reduced many of the rights in criminal procedure established by the Warren Court. It has achieved this end not by flat prohibitions but by its own readings—namely, by drawing distinctions and redefining a handful of essential terms. Even under Warren-era rules, the prosecution was able to introduce at trial evidence that the police, in the absence of a warrant, had found "in plain view." But the Rehnquist Court has enlarged this category by admitting, for example, evidence detected by aerial surveillance using sophisticated cameras. By distinguishing between a mere "stop" and a genuine "arrest" the current Court has also permitted the use of evidence disclosed by police friskings, such as weapons or contraband, that would otherwise have been excluded. It has similarly declared that the "reasonable expectation of privacy" does not cover sealed garbage bags deposited in a dumpster. The Sixth Amendment guarantees an accused person the right "to be confronted with the witnesses against him," but the Court has decided that this right can be waived in cases involving the sexual abuse of children who would be psychologically harmed by having to sit face to face with their presumed victimizer.

Some of these new lines drawn by the Court are quite reasonable, while others seem less so. But this is a side issue; what matters here is that the rights of Americans are creatures of state action. The very scope of our rights against police, prosecutorial, and custodial abuse is established by judicial interpretation, that is, by government performance. The enforcement of these rights by judicial authority over executive-branch officials is merely a secondary illustration of the dependence of individual liberty on state action. The first and most basic way in which publicly funded authorities affect liberty is by defining its scope. The community does not protect any imagined freedoms, but only those which, at any given historical moment, its government, largely through its judiciary, identifies as enforceable rights, and is willing to protect, which is to say fund, as such.

The American system of criminal justice is expensive, in part, because it is designed both to avoid falsely convicting innocent defendants and to prevent lethally armed police officers and prison guards from mistreating even those who are declared guilty. That the costs of these arrangements, indispensable for the protection of basic rights, must be publicly defrayed has theoretical as well as financial significance. Such costs bring into sharp relief the essential dependency of rights-based individualism on state action and social cooperation.

PART II:

WHY RIGHTS CANNOT BE ABSOLUTES

Chapter Five
HOW SCARCITY AFFECTS LIBERTY

JOSHUA DESHANEY WAS BORN IN 1979. His parents were divorced a year later and his father, Randy DeShaney, remarried soon after he was awarded legal custody of the infant. In January 1982, Randy DeShaney's second wife charged her husband with child abuse, alerting the Winnebago County (Wisconsin) Department of Social Services (DSS) that Joshua's father was beating the boy. Officials from DSS interviewed the father, who denied the charges. In January 1983, Joshua was admitted to a local hospital with multiple bruises and abrasions. Suspecting child abuse, the examining doctor notified DSS. Joshua was placed in the temporary custody of the hospital.

Three days later, after conducting an exam, a team of public officials concluded that the evidence of abuse did not warrant keeping Joshua in public custody. A month later, Joshua was again treated for injuries. A DSS caseworker made monthly home visits during which she observed more head wounds. In March 1984, Randy DeShaney beat his four-year-old son so cruelly that the boy lapsed into a coma. Emergency surgery disclosed hemorrhages caused by recurrent blows to the head. Joshua survived but with severe brain damage, and he is expected to spend the rest of his life in an institution for the severely retarded.

Joshua's mother brought suit on his behalf against DSS,

claiming that its failure to provide protection against this sickening brutality constituted a violation of Joshua's fundamental rights under the Constitution. The Supreme Court rejected this claim, asserting that although Joshua's case was undoubtedly tragic, he had suffered no constitutional wrong.[1]

While widely criticized, the DeShaney decision has also found powerful defenders within the American legal community. These defenders divide into two camps. Some echo the Court's own reasoning, alleging that Joshua possessed no constitutional right to state protection. His constitutional rights were not violated because such rights safeguard private individuals exclusively from public officials; they do not entitle people to state protection from their fellow citizens. The Constitution protects individuals from private action only if the government has somehow authorized or encouraged or sponsored the action, or was significantly involved in bringing it about. Since there is no right to affirmative government assistance, and since DSS oversight of child custody cases did not seriously implicate the state in the abusive behavior, no constitutional protection came into play.

Other defenders of this disputed decision take a different line, arguing more pragmatically and not relying on a sharp distinction between negative and positive liberties. Instead of headlining the Constitution's chilly indifference to Joshua's fate, they argue that American courts, for various reasons, cannot effectively manage scarce resources. Instead of alleging that people have no right to affirmative assistance from the state, or that no "state action" was involved, they claim that courts are poorly positioned to make rational decisions about how executive agencies should allocate their budgets and their time. By attending to the difference between these two quite distinct rationales for the controversial DeShaney decision, we can deepen our understanding of the issues raised by the budgetary cost of rights.

Does the Constitution Protect against Privately Inflicted Harms?

The first line of reasoning, articulated by the Court itself, ignores the issue of costs. The due process clause, the Court declared, operates as "a limitation on the State's power to act, not as a guarantee of certain minimal levels of safety and security." The Court added that "its language cannot fairly be extended to impose an affirmative obligation on the State to ensure that [people's] interests do not come to harm. . . . Its purpose was to protect the people from the State, not to ensure that the State protected them from each other." These few words are rich with implications. Behind this grand pronouncement, in fact, lies a comprehensive theory of negative constitutionalism, which implies the following: the Constitution is designed principally to prevent action by federal authorities. It is a giant restraining order imposed by citizens upon their government. Not the First and Fourteenth Amendments alone, but the Constitution as a whole ties the hands of public officials in order to protect the population from tyrannical rule. That is not only its overriding purpose, but also its almost exclusive purpose.

While constitutional rights hamstring public officials, according to this widely accepted view, they place no constraints whatsoever on miscreants out of office. As a result, the Constitution does not *oblige* public officials to protect individuals from private force and fraud, and the government's failure to prevent private wrongs is not a form of state action for which officials could be held judicially accountable.[2]

But the text of the Constitution hardly settles the issue. True, the due process clause bans the state from "depriving" people of life, liberty, or property, but to know whether the state has "deprived" anyone of anything, we need to know what people are entitled to have. If "liberty" includes a right to police protection, then the state deprives people of "liberty" when it fails to provide police protection. If "liberty" includes freedom from private brutality or intrusion, then the state deprives people of "liberty" when it allows people to be subject to private brutality or intrusion. The text is therefore inconclusive. Or suppose it is agreed that the Constitution does not protect people from private action; how much follows from this? Even if the Constitution does not protect people against private acts, it may impose a duty *on the state* to protect private people against private intrusions. The fact that the Constitution applies largely or even exclusively to "the state" does not eliminate this possibility.[3]

Indeed, it is not hard to think of constitutional rights that oblige state action to protect individuals from privately inflicted harms. If a state decided not to protect your property against private trespassers—if, in other words, the state repealed, selectively or entirely, the laws of trespass—a serious question would arise whether the state had "taken" your property by failing to protect you from private trespassers. To "own" property is to have a right to exclude others, and if a state will not affirmatively help you to exclude others, it may well, under existing law, have taken away what you own. Thus, the right to private property may entail a right to government protection via the trespass laws. Or consider the right to contractual liberty. The Constitution protects people against state impairments of contractual obligations. If a state refused to make its courts available to enforce certain contracts, it would probably be taken to be "impairing" contractual rights. The contracts clause therefore has a positive dimension too, insofar as it guarantees an affirmative right to the use of courts (and government resources) to protect contractual guarantees.

Even those who insist that constitutional rights protect citizens exclusively from public authorities—and not at all from each other—are likely to admit that the Thirteenth Amendment is a graphic exception. "Neither slavery nor involuntary servitude . . . shall exist within the United States" prohibits a form of traditionally private behavior. In a way, the ban on slavery can be read as a straightforward ban on private enslavement; it can also be read as a directive to the government, ensuring that government will not permit involuntary servitude.

Other examples of such an obligation are legion. What if Jones sues Smith to enjoin a threatened assault and then Smith bribes the judge, who accordingly rules for Smith? In this case, under existing law, Jones's rights have been violated *because public officials failed to protect him.* And that is only the beginning: in many cases, the government's involvement with private actions has been deemed sufficient to trigger constitutional constraints, even if it appears that private individuals are asking for state help against other private individuals.

Racially restrictive covenants between private buyers and sellers can be challenged under the equal protection clause because private contracts are hollow unless the government makes its full coercive powers available to enforce them.[4] The

use of those coercive powers raises a serious constitutional problem, even in the context of an apparently private real estate deal.
The Fourteenth Amendment prohibits a private lawyer from
using his peremptory challenges to eliminate jurors on the basis
of race; the involvement of the justice system brings the Constitution into play.[5] Political parties, which belong to civil society not to the state, are constitutionally banned from conducting
primaries in a racially discriminatory fashion.[6] Because government is so directly involved in its operation, the First Amendment limits the freedom of Amtrak, a nominally private
corporation, to quash artistic expression at Penn Station.[7] The
Fourteenth Amendment prohibits racial discrimination by a private restaurant that rents space in a municipal parking garage.[8]
Prison authorities can be sued under the Constitution for
injuries inflicted on one prisoner by another if these authorities
demonstrated serious indifference to the inmates' well-being.[9]

Outside of the constitutional context, an affirmative obligation of government to protect private citizens from each other
is a logical consequence of ordinary rights enforcement. Union
members have a right to report the unscrupulous conduct of
union officials. But this right is effectively meaningless unless
the government visibly protects whistle-blowers from violent
reprisals. Indeed, since the enforcement of rights always creates
"losers," the affirmative duty of the government to protect "win-
ners" from acts of private retaliation is a necessary correlate of
every right. A battered wife has a perfectly well established legal
right to report abuse. But what if her husband carries a firearm?
In that case, her right will be a cruel sham unless the city government has spent tax dollars on such protective measures as
shelters for battered women. The individual's right to testify is

likewise hollow unless the government takes upon itself the (costly) obligation of protecting witnesses from retaliation. The $23 million that the Department of Justice spent in 1996 on witness protection programs can be understood in this light.[10] To enforce rights consistently, public authorities must also bring the full force of the law down upon private individuals who try to inflict physical injury upon other private individuals simply because the latter are exercising their rights. This is yet another way in which personal liberty presupposes active government performance—and yet another reason why rights have costs.

Thus, it does not suffice to declare, in a blanket fashion, that American governments, federal and state, are under no "affirmative obligation" to protect American citizens. The Constitution was not designed to wash the government's hands; nor is that an appropriate role for the Supreme Court. It certainly seems reasonable to say that once welfare officials became aware of the abusive behavior of Joshua's father, they were legally obliged to do something about it. If such an obligation existed, then the boy's rights were violated by the state's action and inaction. At the very least, this sort of ruling cannot be precluded by the curious claim that the American government is never under any legal obligation to protect American citizens. A Supreme Court ruling, after all, is not only the disposition of a particular case; it also broadcasts a message to the public about the basic purpose and meaning of the American social contract. Evaluated in this light, the line of reasoning in *DeShaney* is seriously flawed.

The theoretical importance of the case, however, lies in its lessons for the "absoluteness" of rights. Might the Supreme Court have been arguing more narrowly that Joshua's rights were not absolute, because they were subject to budget constraints?

AN ARGUMENT FROM SCARCITY

The second, more pragmatic argument does not reject the view that Joshua had some sort of right to state protection, but simply takes costs, in the sense of competing goods, into account.[11] Although this reasoning was not emphasized in the majority opinion in *DeShaney*, it almost certainly influenced the outcome in the case, because it supplies the simplest and surest route to that outcome. Rights enforcement often does not depend on courts alone. To remedy past rights violations and deter future rights violations, courts must rely on willing cooperation from government agencies, which, in turn, necessarily operate within stringent fiscal and other constraints. In the context of social services, the problem is clear. To deal with potentially boundless problems, departments of social services are endowed with embarrassingly bounded resources, and they must allocate the scant means at their disposal, using their detailed knowledge of the situation on the ground, as they judge most effective. Hard budget constraints imply that some potential victims of child abuse will become actual victims of child abuse, and the state will have done little or nothing about it. This is deplorable, but in an imperfect world of limited resources, it is also inevitable. Taking rights seriously means taking scarcity seriously.

Courts are not well positioned to oversee the tricky process of efficient resource allocation conducted, with more or less skill, by executive agencies, nor are they readily able to rectify past misallocations. Judges do not have the proper training to perform such functions and they necessarily operate with inadequate and biased sources of information. This is why, under American law, Federal Aviation Administration (FAA) agents generally cannot be sued for their unlucky choice of which civilian aircraft to inspect in which sequence, for the courts obviously cannot take upon themselves responsibility for planning the work schedules of government personnel. Faced with a particularly pressing problem, how can a judge measure its urgency compared to that of other social problems competing for governmental attention, and about which he knows virtually nothing? How can judges, in deciding a single case, take account of annual ceilings on government spending? Unlike a legislature, a court is riveted at any one time to a particular case. Because they cannot survey a broad spectrum of conflicting social needs and then decide how much to allocate to each, judges are institutionally obstructed from considering the potentially serious distributive consequences of their decisions. And they cannot easily decide if the state made an error when concluding, before the fact, that its limited resources were most effectively devoted to cases A, B, and C, rather than to case D—even if it turns out that case D involved a calamity like Joshua DeShaney's. (Perhaps cases A, B, and C were also disasters.)

While judges may be perfectly competent to spot egregious violations of rights and even to invalidate egregious misallocations of resources, they cannot intelligently decide, in most such cases, when imaginable remedies are better channeled to other pressing needs. From this perspective, the *DeShaney* case is most charitably understood not as a dramatic pronouncement that the American government owes no protection to American citizens, but rather as a sober recognition that rights have costs, that funds for the protection of the entire array of legal rights must be drawn from the same inevitably limited budgets. In cases of this sort, courts should be very hesitant to substitute their own judgment for that of executive agencies. Courts cannot easily participate in the job of priority-setting and the optimal distribution of scarce resources that the plaintiff in *DeShaney* called upon them to undertake.

This is a fairly plausible defense of the general approach in *DeShaney*, although not a convincing justification of the particular outcome. The evidence of prior knowledge by state authorities was sufficient to implicate them in the brutal deed, and the abuse was so grave, and so likely, that the modest expenditure that would have been required to prevent it could have been constitutionally mandated without creating an imperialistic judiciary liable to substitute its judgment everywhere for that of the executive branch. But the real importance of the case lies in the opposition it raises between a (false) claim that the Constitution creates only negative rights, and a (true) claim that courts are not in a good position to assess claims that involve resource allocation.

What the two rival rationales for the decision show is that the understanding of basic rights, and therefore of the relation of the judiciary to the other branches of government, depends on a prior choice either to ignore costs or to take them into account. In its opinion, the Court paid no heed to the question of scarce public resources. It could justify the state "inaction" it wished to defend as such only by declaring that a child beaten horribly after having been consigned to his cruel father's custody by court order and while under the government's custodial supervision suffered no violation of his basic rights. The result was one of the most shockingly brutal opinions of modern Supreme Court history. Shockingly brutal and altogether unnecessary. For a narrower and more reasonable justification, based partly on cost, was readily at hand, involving the nonabsolute character of rights that depend on expenditures. The *DeShaney* decision thus provides a powerful incitement to explore more deeply the limits that fiscal constraints necessarily impose, and should impose, upon the proper sphere of judicial decision-making.

RHETORIC AND REALITY

Rights are familiarly described as inviolable, preemptory, and conclusive. But these are plainly rhetorical flourishes. Nothing that costs money can be an absolute. No right whose enforcement presupposes a selective expenditure of taxpayer contributions can, at the end of the day, be protected unilaterally by the judiciary without regard to budgetary consequences for which other branches of government bear the ultimate responsibility. Since protection against private violence is not cheap and necessarily draws on scarce resources, the right to such protection, presuming it exists, cannot possibly be uncompromisable or complete. The very same is true of more familiar individual rights to protection against government abuse. For instance, my right to compensation for the taking of my property under the eminent domain power is worthless if the Treasury is empty and unable to pay. If rights have costs, then the enforcement of rights will always be sensitive to the taxpayer's interest in saving money. Rights will regularly be curtailed when available resources dry up, just as they will become susceptible to expansion whenever public resources expand.

Rights are relative, not absolute claims. Attention to cost is simply another pathway, parallel to more heavily traveled routes, to a better understanding of the qualified nature of all rights, including constitutional rights. It should be a useful supplement to more familiar approaches, not least of all because the conventional cost-blind theory of rights has reinforced a widespread misunderstanding of their social function or purpose. Attention to the costs of rights reveals the extent to which rights enforcement, as actually carried out in the United States (and elsewhere), is shot through with trade-offs, including monetary trade-offs. This does not mean that decisions should be made by accountants, only that public officials and democratic citizens must take budgetary costs into account.

Public finance is an ethical science because it forces us to provide a public accounting for the sacrifices that we, as a community, decide to make, to explain what we are willing to relinquish in pursuit of our more important aims. The theory of rights, if it hopes to capture the way a rights regime structures and governs actual behavior, should take this reality into account. Courts that decide on the enforceability of rights claims in specific cases will also reason more intelligently and transparently if they candidly acknowledge the way costs affect the scope, intensity, and consistency of rights enforcement. And legal theory would be more realistic if it examined openly the competition for scarce resources that necessarily goes on among diverse basic rights and also between basic rights and other social values.

Chapter Six

How Rights Differ from Interests

RIGHTS ARE SOMETIMES DESCRIBED AS MORALLY CHARGED and almost irrebuttable claims, to be sharply distinguished from everyday assertions of interest. Whereas interests are always a matter of more or less, thereby implying trade-offs and compromises, rights are a matter of principle, demanding a kind of clinched, unblinking intransigence. At least that is the way many legal theorists and human-rights advocates tend to speak. A similar viewpoint has been memorably articulated by Ronald Dworkin—a leading American theorist of rights—who, in an evocative phrase, portrays rights as "trumps" that can be played in court against government officials.[1]

This metaphor captures an important aspect of American legal reality. Although no right can flatly override all other considerations, rights can nevertheless qualify as "absolute" in a limited sense. When basic rights are at stake, the government cannot casually invoke mundane considerations as justification for non-enforcement. Legal theorists are only following popular preconceptions and ordinary language, then, when they conceptualize rights as claims qualitatively distinct from mere assertions of interest. Extenuating circumstances (such as exorbitant costs or scarce administrative capacities) may easily excuse the government from protecting a mere interest. But these same considerations will excuse the failure to protect a right only under special and highly restricted conditions.

Dworkin has frequently acknowledged the need to balance one right against another and also the occasional necessity of curtailing otherwise important rights in the name of competing social values of sufficient urgency. Rights cannot be overridden by invoking general utility, he writes, but "a state may be justified in overriding or limiting rights on other grounds" and "the most important . . . of these other grounds invokes the notion of competing rights that would be jeopardized if the right in question were not limited."[2] Freedom of the press may perhaps be restricted by the right to privacy or freedom from malicious libel. Contrariwise, freedom of the press can be expanded by contracting the right to sue for libel. The right to engage in collective bargaining requires the legal abolition of the right to make yellow-dog contracts, whereby workers once "voluntarily" agreed not to join a union. And so forth.

The curtailing of civil liberties to combat terrorism is unquestionably lamentable, but such trade-offs have been made in the past and will no doubt be made again. Although it should have done so, "strict scrutiny" did not in fact prevent the Court from giving its blessing to the flagrantly discriminatory internment of Japanese-Americans in World War II.[3] And there is little guarantee that similar infringements will not occur when pertinent reasons arise that again seem convincing to judges.

The need for swift governmental action is a commonly accepted rationale for overriding important rights. For example, property can be seized without prior notice (an action that would ordinarily violate due process of law) if a shipment of pharmaceuticals has been dangerously adulterated or if a vehicle transporting contraband is about to escape the grasp of the police. Freedom of information can be restricted, or defined in a limited way, on the grounds not only of national security but also to protect sensitive data about government personnel. Under emergency conditions, freedom of movement can be legally curtailed to prevent the spread of highly contagious fatal diseases. And the right to ride a motorcycle without a helmet can be abolished, partly because of the medical and rehabilitation costs such activity imposes on the community as a whole.

A large part of lawyering involves discovering judicially acceptable excuses for actions or omissions that would otherwise be deemed unlawful or unacceptable. As the category "excusable homicide" suggests, even the most socially unacceptable behavior can be justified, as a matter of law, in special circumstances (such as self-defense). Mitigating factors can be invoked to justify governmental as well as private action. What the rights-as-trumps view implies is only that a government that curtails civil liberties must persuasively invoke important public interests. To violate central constitutional values, the state should have even weightier values on its side.

But while the rights-as-trumps view is perfectly at home with the notion that rights occasionally clash with other rights and with other public interests as well, so that judicial balancing is often required, it neglects the idea that rights cannot be absolute because their enforcement depends on the timely delivery of limited public money to the agents charged with enforcing them. Some conflicts among rights stem from a common dependency of all rights on limited budgetary outlays. Financial limits alone exclude the possibility of all basic rights being enforced maximally at the same time. Rights invariably demand or imply trade-offs of a financial sort. And expenditure patterns will to some extent be determined politically. Attending to costs helps explain why property rights clash with property rights, why the local police department cannot protect Jones's dilapidated home adequately if it has already committed its sole stakeout team to guard Smith's luxurious estate.

To be sure, some basic rights, such as freedom of speech or the right to vote, may not be bought and sold on the open market; the ban on trading political rights is designed partly to ensure that political power is not concentrated in any individual or group. So rights are not commodities in a simple sense. But when the price soars, rights enforcement necessarily becomes more selective. We can obtain costly goods and services only by relinquishing something else of value. The world of value is complex and the world of available possibilities is larger than the world of co-available possibilities. There is nothing cynical or degrading about admitting as much or acknowledging that this pattern applies to basic rights as well as to ordinary commodities. Of course, it does not follow that rights must be tossed along with everything else into a gigantic cost-benefit calculating machine created and operated by economists.

Although it is theoretically misleading to portray rights as absolutes, such a description can be defended as psychologically and rhetorically useful. Civil libertarians, like politicians, used-car salesmen, and advertising executives, are keenly aware that exaggeration has a mnemonic function, and they know by experience that their uncompromising phraseology often pays off. Hyperbole can draw special attention to what they see as crying needs, thereby increasing the chance that citizens and representatives will treat certain interests with exceptional sensitivity and seriousness. Perhaps a (misleading) emphasis on the absolute character of free speech will stiffen the spine of citizens and representatives when the pressure for (unjustified) censorship is especially great. But overstatement can create problems too, and an insistence that rights are absolute may lead to the over-protection of some rights to the detriment of others that have an even greater claim. And since political attention, too, is a scarce resource, the more time officials lavish on one claim, the less time they have for another.

Defeasibility is an inescapable characteristic of all legal rights, including constitutional rights. Another important reason, apart from costs, why legal rights must always be subject to curtailment or limitation is also worth revisiting: rights are, in reality, legal powers that can be exercised over others. Powers can always be misused. Rights must be subject to restrictions in order to prevent their exploitation for wrongful ends. For instance, the right to self-defense is well established in American law, but it is justifiable only because, or to the extent that, courts keep an eye out for its abuse. You cannot claim to have acted in self-defense, for example, if you were not seriously endangered. Similarly, the rights of a stockholder to sue a company's management can be used to harass and eventually to obtain a handsome bribe for dropping the case. The possibility of abusive suits must be taken into account by legislators and judges who determine the conditions under which the right to sue fails. The American legal system makes continuous remedial and compensatory adjustments to handle the unintended side effects that necessarily occur whenever the government hands individuals the discretionary right to wield the public power, to dip into the public purse.

But—it will be asked—are not some human interests intrinsic and not merely instrumental goods? While some things are valuable merely as means, are not other things good in themselves, because of the good things that they, on balance, bring into being? True, freedom of speech serves to improve the quality of public decision-making and to reduce the level of government corruption. But is it not also valued for its own sake, simply because censorship is an indignity, an insult to human autonomy? The answer is yes: some interests do have intrinsic value. But even intrinsic goods have costs; they cannot exist without public effort and a substantial expenditure of resources. Protecting rights that are valued for their own sake will entail dangers, downsides, unintended side effects, opportunity costs, and other troubles, for there are few gains without losses. Thus, the right to a hearing serves dignitary functions and is not designed just to ensure accurate fact-finding. But if it is very expensive to hold elaborate hearings, government may not be required to hold elaborate hearings. And the visitation rights of grandparents on the side of the noncustodial parent may seem "sacred" in a way, and certainly such rights are not of merely instrumental value; but such rights are regularly obliterated in American jurisdictions in cases of adoption, out of concern for the countervailing interests of the child.

Indeed, the rights of Americans are constantly expanding and contracting under the impact of legislative and adjudicative action. Rights are interests that, politically and judicially, are highly valued at that moment; but they are not merely that. Within American legal culture, rights are interests of a special kind. Attention to the cost of rights does not render meaningless the fundamental liberal distinction between interests and rights. "Rights talk" is essential because it raises the threshold of justification for interfering with interests deemed especially important.

When rights are at issue, some arguments are not merely insufficiently weighty but altogether inadmissible. This is true in private law as well as constitutional law. The debtor cannot legally refuse to pay his debt because his creditor is an apostate, although he can refuse to pay, under certain conditions, if the product he received proves defective. Analogously, our system of religious liberty does not allow government to suppress a minority's religious practices because the minority's god is not the true God, although it can ban the consumption of hallucinogens in specific contexts. Our system of political liberty does not deprive people of the vote because incumbents fear how people will vote. Our system of free expression does not allow government to regulate ideas simply because officials or citizens think those ideas are wrong or dangerous, but it can regulate them for other reasons. And once we identify the category of permissible and impermissible reasons for action in any particular system, we are well on our way toward understanding what rights, as interests of a special type, mean in practice.

For example, the Winnebago County DSS could not justify its failure to protect a child from his father's brutality by invoking racial or religious considerations. It could not say, "We protect white children but not black children." Whether or not the Constitution obliges the government to protect individuals from private harms, its use of such a justification would have been, without any question, absolutely forbidden. Similarly, a court cannot deny child custody to a divorced white mother simply because she is now cohabiting with a black man. That justification for state action is blocked. America's rights regime is

"absolutist" in this sense: it rules out certain reasons uncondi-
tionally while proscribing actions and inactions only condition-
ally.

Formulated differently, rights are regulatory, not prohibitive.
American courts do not ordinarily defend constitutional rights
simply by barring government actions as unlawful. What courts
do, rather, is to require that the level or branch of government
involved provide legitimate and substantial grounds for restrictions imposed and actions undertaken or omitted. This is one
way that the American judiciary contributes to democratic
accountability—compelling legislative and executive authorities, whenever they infringe upon the interests currently denominated as rights, publicly to articulate the legitimacy and
importance of the goals they are pursuing and the appropriateness of the means they select. Rights rule off-limits certain justifications for action or inaction.[4]

To avoid misinterpreting rights as un-overrideable vetoes
blocking the path of policy, we could choose to emphasize the
perennial need to balance among conflicting interests. But the
"balancing" metaphor is just as misleading as the vague notion
that rights are absolutes. If all rival claims must be weighed
against one another, then claims of right are not essentially different from claims of interest. But this is a simplification, for
when a right is in play, government cannot justify non-enforcement simply by claiming that some discernible interests lie on
the other side.

This is a familiar phenomenon in daily life. If a friend tells
you something in confidence, you may breach the confidence if
doing so is necessary to save that friend's life; you may not blab
simply because it is fun to gossip about your friend's problems.

If a friend is getting married, you may regretfully decide not to attend the wedding, perhaps, if your child is sick and you cannot find substitute care. But you may not decline simply because there is a swell sitcom on television at the hour of the ceremony. Our ordinary decision-making is routinely based on the exclusion of certain reasons as utterly irrelevant, rather than merely unimportant. So outside the law, decision-making is touched by "absoluteness" in this sense and is not merely a matter of balancing.

The same is true of decisions made in the legal sphere. The law's elevation of a certain subset of interests into legally enforceable rights usually deletes, for the time being, certain justifications from the menu of acceptable reasons for interfering with them. To the extent that certain justifications are inadmissible, the right does indeed work, for restricted purposes, in absolutist fashion. But because more persuasive justifications always remain admissible, rights never qualify as uncompromisable when the would-be rights violator comes up with legitimate and sufficiently weighty grounds for neglecting them. Scarcity of resources is a legitimate, however regrettable, reason for failure to protect rights. The two rationales for *DeShaney*, even though neither is convincing in the end, provide a useful illustration of this powerful truth.

AMONG CONSTITUTIONAL RIGHTS, freedom of speech is one of the most precious. It is worth protecting even, or rather especially, in extreme circumstances, for free speech makes it much more likely that the violation of other rights will be reported. Alongside its many psychological, moral, artistic, religious, and economic functions, liberty of expression is an essential precondition for democratic self-government. It helps ensure political accountability, mop up governmental corruption, drag into the daylight abuses of power, and improve the quality of policy-making by enlisting suggestions and criticisms from specialists out of office as well as from the public at large. In less-developed countries, freedom of speech can even help prevent famines.[5] This is why freedom of expression and communication is sometimes described as the liberty on which all other liberties depend. No surprise that free speech has a special place in American legal culture and has been frequently styled as uninfringeable.

Nevertheless, like other forms of public behavior—which always entails the risk of mutual harm among private individuals and groups—speech is regulated every day, and with good reason. A right is a power, and any power can be misused. Americans would certainly be worse off if the U. S. government dealt with free speech as if it were untouchable. There are (reasonable) laws on the books restricting perjury, attempted bribery, price-fixing, fraudulent and misleading commercial advertising, child pornography, conspiracy, threats to assassinate the president, and many other forms of speech. Not even free-speech purists favor abolishing all such restrictions in the name of individual freedom and autonomy. In practice, doctrinaire extremists in this area are merely trying to shift, usually relatively slightly, the line that political and judicial authorities have drawn when regulating communication and expression. Those who claim that they are "free-speech absolutists" do not really mean it. Some constraints on speech are merely common sense, even in a nation strongly committed to freedom of expression. We would be less free if freedom of speech were treated as a preemptory claim immune to regulation, even when other important interests or rights are in jeopardy.

But what principles help us separate constitutionally protected speech from constitutionally unprotected speech? Constitutional lawyers have been extraordinarily creative in elaborating such principles. But in the United States, whenever the right to free speech is widely perceived to have socially unacceptable consequences (including the undesirable social costs of perjury and the other illicit speech acts listed above), this right is abridged without much embarrassment. Freedom of expression can and will be compromised when the side effects of the unlimited exercise of this right are perceived to be exceptionally harmful. Some such infringements are morally dismaying, but others are not, and in any case they are politically unavoidable. Freedom of speech will be intruded on when, in the eyes of the judiciary, the reasons for doing so have sufficient legitimacy and weight, and less drastic means are not readily (which may mean inexpensively) available. Conversely, a constitutional right prevails when publicly and judicially acceptable justifications for intruding upon it cannot be found.

The controversial issue of flag burning illustrates the point. The government cannot regulate flag burning on the ground that public officials hate protesters, or believe that this is an especially heinous and unpatriotic act, or fear that many people will be upset by an expression of outrage against the symbol of the country's nationhood. But government can regulate flag burning on the neutral grounds of protecting private property from destruction. Freedom of speech is classified as a precious right rather than an ordinary interest because of the sharply restricted conditions under which it can be compromised.

At the time when the First Amendment was adopted, relatively few of its framers had a particularly radical idea of free speech. Most of them agreed that orderly government was an inherently fragile and vulnerable creation that must be protected, in certain circumstances, from the potentially corrosive power of words. Certainly the framers did not intend to ban regulation of anything that could come from a mouth or a pen. There is much dispute about what the framers particularly believed, but no one can deny that the current conception of the free speech principle is far broader than the understanding held by its authors.[6] The meaning of free speech in the United States began to evolve in the 1790s and has been developing ever since. Its scope, at any given time, has always depended upon changing interpretations by a changing Court. Today, spending money to elect a candidate is a form of constitutionally protected free speech, whereas burning one's draft card is not. There is nothing inevitable about this dispensation; right or wrong, it is literally a matter of interpretation.

Today, the government generally may not punish speech because people are offended by the ideas that it contains. Some individuals and groups may be grievously offended by the ideas expressed in a communist tract. But even if the moral injury is large—even if people become suicidally depressed from prolonged exposure to offensive ideas—offense ordinarily does not count as a legitimate basis for public action, at least not in the United States. In the context of speech, outrage at the content of expressed ideas is flatly excluded as a ground for governmental regulation. Whatever the consequences, offense is usually an unacceptable reason for restricting speech. Even the controversial restrictions on sexual harassment in the workplace are justified as a way of preventing employment discrimination, not offense.

Freedom of speech implies far more than a right against direct censorship of disfavored opinions. Every tyrant knows that he can effectively stifle annoying public protests, even without explicitly banning expression as such, simply by cordoning off arenas where demonstrations and rallies are likely to be staged. Hence the right to free speech, protected under American law, includes a right of access to public forums and, as a logical consequence, a right to ensure that certain public places—such as public streets and parks—are kept open and available for expressive activity.

In this particular way, freedom of speech does not simply require that the government adopt a hands-off approach, for maintaining open public spaces will ordinarily entail nontrivial public expenses, presupposing a degree of compulsory taxing and spending. The right to set up a soapbox and enter a publicly subsidized space where listeners can gather and supporters parade imposes costs on some citizens for the benefit of others. Indeed, the Supreme Court has strongly suggested that the government cannot charge the immediate users of freedom of speech, such as protesters in a public park, for the expenses for speech-related activities.[7] All taxpayers, including those who are not especially free-speaking or interested in protest, must pay. Strollers do not need to purchase tickets to walk around in most public parks. Similarly, legal rights are subsidized by taxes levied on the community at large, not by fees paid by the individuals who happen to be exercising them at the moment. Because this is a necessary, not an accidental arrangement, redistribution in the field of rights protection seems to be inevitable.

The implications may be profound, for in stark contrast to its reasoning in the *DeShaney* case, the Court has indicated that government subsidies, in the free speech context, may well be constitutionally required. How could the Court distinguish the cases? Perhaps what it aims to say is that freedom of speech, properly understood, means that publicly subsidized expressive arenas must be assigned a high budgetary priority no matter what other claims are competing for community resources. That may be implied by classifying freedom of speech as a right rather than merely an interest of American citizens. But if this is the Court's point, its cost-free style of argumentation prevents it from formulating its conclusion in terms clear enough to invite constructive criticism, or from elucidating its deeper assumptions and spelling out the wider implications of its approach.

Chapter Seven
ENFORCING RIGHTS MEANS DISTRIBUTING RESOURCES

THE RIGHT TO VOTE is no more costless than any other right. Putting aside all private expenditures for political campaigns, the 1996 elections probably cost the American taxpayer somewhere between $300 million and $400 million.[1] Of course, accurate nationwide statistics are difficult to come by. This is partly because almost all of the public costs of running elections are borne by states and municipalities. Federal spending is minimal. State taxpayers pay the costs of printing ballots, registration materials, and voter guides, while municipal taxpayers defray the expenses of staffing and maintaining polling stations. Voting booths must be kept in working order, bans on advertising near the polling stations must be enforced, and vote fraud must be deterred and detected. (Running a mayoral election, it should be noted, costs a city no less than running a senatorial or presidential election. Once the initial investment in holding an election has been made, the additional costs of adding more candidates and ballot initiatives is minimal.)

As the legal philosopher Hans Kelsen once remarked, "to the citizen's right of vote corresponds the duty of the election officer."[2] And that election officer, he might have added, will ordinarily be paid. Polling stations must be opened in various locations, geographically distributed to give approximately equal access to all voters. Under certain conditions, states are constitutionally obliged to make absentee voting procedures available to inmates awaiting trial or convicted of misdemeanors.[3] And local and state governments must use general tax revenues to put into place all the preconditions for fair elections, since they cannot condition the right to vote on the payment of an individualized poll tax or user fee. Such a governmentally managed subsidy is necessarily redistributive.

Perhaps because the costs of elections vary so greatly from city to city, state officials seem strangely reluctant to engage in a thorough accounting. Available figures are nonetheless suggestive. In Massachusetts, a state law passed prior to the 1996 presidential elections mandated longer hours for polling stations. Implementing this tiny amendment to the law cost Massachusetts taxpayers $800,000.[4] In California, where a study of electoral expenses was commissioned by the state government, the cost of any statewide election (whether presidential, senatorial, gubernatorial, etc.) runs around $45–50 million. This is also true for any referendum requiring a separate ballot. Printing and mailing costs for voter guides alone, including those printed in Spanish as well as English, can range from $3 million to $12 million. In California, the cost per voter is estimated to run from $2 to $5, depending on each municipality's voting system.[5]

Today, the right to vote would be unconstitutionally infringed if courts were not permitted to outlaw impermissible racial gerrymandering. The money for such remedial activities and, more generally, for organizing and carrying out free and fair elections is extracted from both willing and unwilling taxpayers, from voters and nonvoters alike. Voting would be a very different act, would bear a very different social meaning, if voters alone had to pay a fee to defray the public costs of conducting an election, instead of all taxpayers having to pay. That a modest form of compulsory redistribution is involved is obviously not an argument against the right to vote. Indeed, we are so used to the taxing and spending presupposed by representative government that we simply take it for granted.

If both the right to free speech and the right to vote require public expenditures, presuppose redistributive decisions, and are relative rather than absolute goods, the same is likely to be true of other rights as well. The Fourth Amendment confers protection against unreasonable searches and seizures. It obliges the government to perform a service that can, under some conditions, be extremely expensive—namely, to monitor police behavior accurately and to deter misbehavior by a fair but also swift and reliable system of punishment. And if citizens are to hold police officers accountable for their actions, they must also finance the procedural protections that accused officers, too, deserve. As a practical matter, resources extracted from the taxpayer will have to be targeted to ensure that lethally armed police officers neither behave unlawfully nor are falsely convicted of behaving unlawfully. Private liberty depends on the quality of public institutions.

THOSE WHO ACCLAIM RIGHTS as trumps sometimes also construe them as barriers defending the most cherished individual interests against a repressive or meddlesome community. Individuals invoke their rights to fend off the majority. Rights protect individuals from mob rule. There is some truth to this antimajoritarian idea. We are all familiar with the lone dissident fighting for his freedom to engage in nonconformist speech and the

religious outsider seeking to practice her religion despite majority bigotry and intolerance. But are rights adequately described
as claims that the solitary individual raises against the community in which he or she was born and bred? The idea that rights
are erected against the community is obviously too simple, for
rights are interests on which we, as a community, have bestowed
special protection, usually because they touch upon "the public
interest"—that is, because they involve either the interests of the
collectivity as a whole or the fair treatment of various members
of the community. By recognizing, protecting, and financing
rights, the collectivity fosters what are widely construed to be
the deeper interests of its members.

Property rights encourage individuals to improve their property by allowing owners to capture the benefits of improvement.
This arrangement is a social one created for social purposes; it
has a perceptibly positive effect on a nation's real estate and
capital stock. Other seemingly individual rights are likewise
collectively conferred, designed, reshaped, interpreted, adjusted,
and enforced to promote what are widely seen as collective interests. They are protected by public institutions, including legislatures and courts, for collective reasons. Admittedly, and
importantly, rights may operate in some sense "against" the
collectivity once they are vested in individuals. Government
may not confiscate property simply because a majority wants to
do so. But even in such cases, rights are guaranteed in the first
instance both by and for the collectivity. Since it has no existence
apart from the individuals who compose it, a collectivity can
define, confer, interpret, and protect rights only if it is politically well organized and only if it can act in a coherent manner
through the instrumentality of an accountable government.

Arguing that rights serve collective purposes, the philosopher Joseph Raz remarks, "If I were to choose between living in a society which enjoys freedom of expression, but not having the right myself, or enjoying the right in a society which does not have it, I would have no hesitation in judging that my own personal interest is better served by the first option."[6] The right to free expression benefits individuals largely because of its social consequences: diminishing the risk of ill-considered government action, promoting scientific progress, encouraging the dissemination of knowledge, and ensuring that government oppression or abuse will sometimes be met by clamorous protest. Individuals in a society without free speech suffer most from what the lack of freedom does to that society. So, too, are both individual and social welfare promoted by the rights to a fair trial, freedom from unreasonable searches and seizures, and freedom of religion. In all these cases, the relevant right helps secure goods for many people beyond those who personally assert it at the moment. This is one reason why most rights are funded out of general revenues rather than by narrowly targeted user fees.

Chapter Eight
WHY TRADEOFFS ARE INESCAPABLE

WITH THESE WORDS, President Franklin D. Roosevelt proposed a Second Bill of Rights in 1944:

> We have accepted, so to speak, a second Bill of Rights under which a new basis of security and prosperity can be established for all—regardless of station, race, or creed.
>
> The right to a useful and remunerative job in the industries or shops or farms or mines of the Nation;
>
> The right to earn enough to provide adequate food and clothing and recreation;
>
> The right of every farmer to raise and sell his products at a return which will give him and his family a decent living; . . .
>
> The right of every family to a decent home;
>
> The right to adequate medical care and the opportunity to achieve and enjoy good health;
>
> The right to adequate protection against the economic fears of old age, sickness, accident, and unemployment;
>
> The right to a good education.[1]

HALF A CENTURY LATER, people all over the world are still debating what rights belong in the Constitution. Should a Constitution, for example, protect the right to social security? How should we understand the rights to housing, welfare, and food?

Should there be a constitutional right to employment? Roosevelt's detractors scoff at his attempt to put such "rights" on the same footing as the classical freedoms from government interference. They strenuously object to the very idea of constitutionalizing such rights, even though the International Covenant on Economic, Social, and Cultural Rights (adopted by the United Nations in 1966), which has been copied verbatim into many new post-communist constitutions, does treat minimal social and economic guarantees as if they were equivalent to civil liberties and political rights.[2]

It is familiarly said that welfare rights and other social and economic guarantees are aspirational or open-ended. There is never a point at which they are completely protected. This characterization is correct, but it should not be made with the assumption that old-fashioned rights, such as freedom from unreasonable searches and seizures or police brutality, are fully enforceable. Those who object to welfare rights because they cost money should not assume that property rights can be fully safeguarded, for the conventional contrast between aspirational welfare rights and limited property rights does not survive scrutiny. Our freedom from government interference is no less budget-dependent than our entitlement to public assistance. Both freedoms must be interpreted. Both are implemented by public officials who, drawing on the public purse, have a good deal of discretion in construing and protecting them.

The argument that poor nations can afford the first generation but not the second generation of rights is not wholly misdirected, but, as stated, it is far too simple. If first-generation rights are taken seriously, and if they turn out to be quite expensive, truly poor nations cannot afford them either. They cannot ensure that a right to a fair trial is always respected in practice, just as it is not always respected in poor neighborhoods in the United States, notwithstanding this country's historically unprecedented wealth. All rights are open-ended for the simple reason that rights have costs and hence can never be perfectly or completely protected. All rights are aspirational.

Should nations—whether poor or rich—constitutionalize social and economic guarantees? This is not only a philosophical question about the essential nature of rights as such, but also an acutely pragmatic one, raising issues of institutional competence and also of public finance that should be decided by considering available resources, predictable side effects, and competing goals. Philosophical arguments may show that minimal guarantees deserve to be classed among basic human interests.[3] It is perfectly obvious that people cannot lead decent lives without certain minimal levels of food, shelter, and health care. But calling the crying need for public assistance "basic" may not get us very far. A just society would ensure that its citizens have food and shelter; it would try to guarantee adequate medical care; it would strive to offer good education, good jobs, and a clean environment. But which of these goals should it pursue by creating rights, legal or even constitutional? This is a question that cannot be answered by abstract theory alone; everything depends on context.

Those opposed to constitutionalizing welfare rights usually argue along the following lines. A constitution is a legal document with limited tasks. If a country tries to make legally binding and judicially enforceable everything that a decent society requires, its constitution risks losing its coherence. If Americans created expensive constitutional rights to housing and health

care, which depend on the state of the economy, we would over-
load our Bill of Rights. Indeed, by labeling as "constitutional
rights" valuable services that we sometimes cannot afford to
deliver, we may even cheapen traditional American liberties in
the eyes of citizens, who will begin to see constitutional rights as
claims to be honored or not, depending on resources available
at the time.

These points have some force. But since all rights depend on
the state of the economy and public finances, the decision to
constitutionalize or not to constitutionalize welfare rights cannot be made on such grounds alone. Not a single right valued
by Americans can be reliably enforced if the Treasury is empty.
All rights are protected only to a degree, and this degree
depends partly on budgetary decisions about how to allocate
scarce public resources. If rights have costs then, like it or not,
"politics is trumps,"[4] to use political scientist B. Guy Peters's
aphoristic reminder of the inevitable role of political choice in
the creation of public budgets.

Some countries (Germany is an example) have constitutionalized certain kinds of welfare rights without noticeably cheap-
ening freedom of the press or procedural guarantees. By contrast,
the American welfare state relies almost entirely on statute, not
the Constitution. But there is less to this distinction than meets
the eye. The demand for welfare rights arises forcefully out of
modern economies and societies. For the most part, the level of
protection welfare rights receive is determined politically, not
judicially, whether such rights are officially constitutionalized
or not.

One might think that in developing nations second-generation constitutional rights to minimum welfare guarantees are

not desirable, because they would cost a great deal more than first-generation rights to more familiar liberties (a distinction of degree), because they would give the wrong kind of power to the judiciary, because they would not produce adequate social returns, or because they would send the wrong signal about the basic point of government. These are practical issues. But to consider first-generation rights "priceless" and second-generation rights "costly" is not only imprecise, it also encourages the fantasy that the courts can generate their own power and impose their own solutions, whether or not the legislative or executive branches happen to support them. The American judiciary may or may not be the forum of basic principle, but it is certainly constructed and buttressed by the extractive branches of government, which provide the fiscal wherewithal to nourish and house the judiciary and, generally, to keep it alive and functioning. To focus on the cost of rights is therefore to shed light on an important and poorly understood aspect of the American separation of powers.

While many rights appear in the American Constitution, it is a mistake to think that their specific content is chiseled in constitutional granite. During no thirty-year period is the concrete meaning of our basic constitutional rights likely to remain constant. As old social problems fade away and new social problems spring up, the way rights are construed naturally evolves. To draw attention to how the rights of Americans are ceaselessly changing is emphatically not to defend relativism, to say that basic human interests differ wildly across cultures, or to imply that governments should define rights however they wish. But as a descriptive matter, rights are in important respects context-dependent. The way they are interpreted and applied shifts with changing circumstances and with advances or retreats in knowledge. Freedom of speech is a revealing example. What freedom of speech means in contemporary American constitutional jurisprudence is not what it meant fifty or one hundred years ago. The significance and implications of First Amendment rights have not stood still in the past and will surely continue to change in the future.

Many reasons account for this ceaseless and unpredictable evolution. Judgments about issues of value, fact, and harm change with time and place. But another source of variation is more mundane, for rights are rooted in the most shifting of all political soils, that of the annual budgetary process, a process thick with ad hoc political compromises. Built on such shifting terrain, rights are bound to be less indefeasible than the desire for legal certainty might lead us to wish. To take account of this unstable reality, therefore, we ought not to conceive of rights as floating above time and place, or as absolute in character. It is more realistic and more productive to define rights as individual powers deriving from membership in, or affiliation with, a political community, and as selective investments of scarce collective resources, made to achieve common aims and to resolve what are generally perceived to be urgent common problems.

The constitutions of Germany, Mexico, Brazil, Hungary, and Russia include, in various forms, a right to a safe and healthy environment. (The extent to which these rights can be enforced through the court systems in these countries is debatable, but it is modest even in the best of cases.) In the United States, too, people have argued vigorously on behalf of such a legally entrenched third-generation right at the national level. They urge that the interest in environmental protection is systematically undervalued in ordinary political processes, and that future generations deserve protection against environmental degradation perpetrated by those now living, who, being myopic and self-interested, are all too likely to act as faithless trustees. As theoretical arguments, these claims have considerable force.

Yet even if the interest in environmental protection were promoted to the status of a judicially enforceable right, it would still be protected only to some degree, and its public costs would grow in direct proportion to the degree of protection afforded. Environmental protection is a very costly business. Not even the Superfund (designed to ensure clean-up of abandoned toxic-waste dumps) is unlimited. Rescuing endangered species—poached and poisoned to the point of extinction—can be expensive. And these are only two examples. In the United States, more than fifty million people continue to live in areas that fail to meet national ambient-air-quality standards. Although the nation already expends more than $130 billion per year on environmental regulation, it is not clear if our environmental regulations represent, in their current form, the most intelligent uses of limited resources.

In environmental protection, increasing attention is being paid to the phenomenon of "health-health trade-offs," which occur when regulation of one risk simultaneously increases another risk.[5] An absolutist or single-minded approach to specific risks may well increase overall or aggregate risks. If the personal interest in being free from sulfur dioxide, which is certainly not trivial, were treated as an absolute right, the result would be a range of additional social problems, including new environmental problems; perhaps elimination of sulfur dioxide would lead to more dangerous replacements, or create serious waste-disposal problems. Inevitably, resources devoted to some problems will draw away resources from others; a government that channels the lion's share of its environmental resources to clean up hazardous-waste dumps will find itself penniless to protect clean air or clean water. Single-minded protection against highly salient environmental risks may compromise larger and longer-run environmental interests. Aggressive protection against dangers from nuclear power accidents may increase the price, and decrease the supply, of nuclear power, and in that way increase dependence on fossil fuels, which create environmental problems of their own. A no-compromise attitude will therefore produce confusion and arbitrariness and may, on balance, disserve the very rights it intends to promote.

To be enacted and implemented sensibly, enforceable rights to a safe and healthy environment would have to channel limited resources to the highest priority problems. Supreme Court Justice Stephen Breyer has vigorously argued that poor priority-setting is a central obstacle to good regulation.[6] This suggests that anyone entrusted with respecting environmental rights will have to make hard decisions about what problems and which groups have an overriding claim on collective resources. A key goal of the legal system ought to be to overcome the problem of selective attention, a general problem that emerges whenever participants focus on one aspect of an issue to the exclusion of other aspects. In a way, an emphasis on the cost of rights can be understood as a response to the problem of selective attention. "Health-health" trade-offs are paralleled by "environment-environment" trade-offs, as when protection of clean air increases solid-waste disposal problems, and the "rights-rights" trade-offs that arise when, for example, use of the legal system to protect environmental quality makes fewer resources available to protect, say, against criminal violence.

The environment is for the most part collectively enjoyed and, if the air gets a good deal cleaner or less clean, many or most of us will be positively or negatively affected. This point is important, for any general "right" to environmental quality could entail an individual plaintiff's capacity to dictate at least minimal levels of water and air quality for thousands or even millions of people. Environmental interests, recast as judicially enforceable rights, could have serious collective consequences on both the cost and benefit sides. They would certainly involve a redistribution of resources from some people to others in the form of taxation, and an additional redistribution at the point of expenditure.

So what would be the effect, in the United States, of creating a constitutional right to environmental protection? Some environmentalists say that a safe environment is an absolute good and should be provided "whatever it takes." But safety is a relative, not an absolute, concept. The question is "How safe?" rather than "Safe or not?" Achieving higher levels of safety requires both private and public expenditures, and perhaps those expenditures are best made elsewhere. If it were enforceable in court, a constitutional right to a safe environment could entrust judges with the job of identifying the point at which such a right has been adequately respected. Are courts better equipped to carry out this task than they are to micromanage the Winnebago County DSS? For one thing, they lack the fact-finding capacity in the environmental arena that would justify their making particular allocative decisions. For another, they are not politically accountable. Equally important, they lack the overview of the tangle of economic and environmental issues that would be necessary, at a minimum, for deciding rationally that one policy should be chosen over an alternative.

The professional incapacity of judges does not, by itself, establish that the palpable interest of a nation's citizens in environmental quality has no conceivable place in a constitution. Perhaps such a "right" should be created and simply construed as a directive to the legislature, not to the courts. Perhaps such a "right" would not be judicially enforceable at all but would instead be useful as a weapon in political debate. Perhaps such a quasi-right or symbolic right could be designed not to ensure any particular outcome but instead to flag the importance and denounce the government's disregard of environmental interests. Perhaps courts could play a modest and appropriate role by calling public attention to cases in which political actors have conspicuously defaulted on their responsibilities—as the Supreme Court should have done in *DeShaney* itself.

Whether a particular nation should enshrine a right to environmental quality in its constitution remains debatable. Under current conditions, with an active, vigorous, and frequently successful environmental movement, a constitutional amendment of this kind probably would not make sense for the United States. But if third-generation rights ever become judicially enforceable, they will be less distinctive than both critics and proponents seem to expect. From the perspective of public finance, the three generations of rights occupy a continuum, rather than being radically distinct kinds of claims. Extending the insight of Justice Breyer, we might even say that poor priority-setting afflicts the entire domain of rights enforcement. The question is always "How well protected?" rather than "Protected or not?" Anyone entrusted with enforcing legal rights will have to make hard decisions about what problems, and which groups, have an overriding claim on collective resources in particular circumstances.

Those charged with monitoring child custody cases are not the only ones who must bear this burden. Are citizens who are subjected to police abuse in a position altogether different from that in which Joshua DeShaney found himself? Consider their right to be free from unreasonable searches and seizures. Although constitutionally entrenched and undoubtedly a right, this right cannot be absolute in the sense of uncompromisable. No right can be uncompromisable if its scope hinges upon the shifting judicial interpretation of a word as vague and indeterminate as "unreasonable." Even more importantly, the Fourth Amendment right cannot be absolute unless the public is willing to invest the enormous amounts necessary to ensure that it is seldom violated in practice. The fact that the Fourth Amendment is violated so regularly shows that the public is not willing to make that investment.

A police officer told one of the authors that the Fourth Amendment does not give him "much trouble," because "I don't violate the Fourth Amendment unless I say I violated the Fourth Amendment, and I never say I violated the Fourth Amendment." Monitoring officials cannot do their job effectively unless they can obtain reliable information about misbehavior from sources independent of the officials suspected of abuse: officers on duty have a palpable incentive to knead and color the facts when crafting reports for higher officials, including the judiciary. Exorbitant information costs sometimes make the price of protecting even the most precious rights prohibitively high. Although the right to be free from unreasonable searches and seizures is constitutionally guaranteed, it is violated every day in practice. The politics of budget-making is one reason why.

Not only is the right to private property financed by the community, but the indisputably nonabsolute character of that right is a function of, among other factors, cost. What would it take to ensure that the rights of owners were never violated? The degree to which property rights are actually enforced varies with historical circumstances, political resolve, and state capacities, including meager or bountiful tax revenues. In protecting private property, a liberal polity (even one free of corruption and racial bias) necessarily husbands its scarce resources with an eye to competing social purposes. Some funds must be held in reserve, for instance, for the enforcement and protection of other kinds of rights. To enforce rights fairly, the government cannot expend its entire annual budget on protecting the property rights of a few individuals during the first few months of the budgetary year. Nor would any property owner be willing to hand over 100 percent of his income and wealth to have 100 percent perfect police protection of his (thereby non-existent) estate.

The decision about how thoroughly to protect property rights overloads the fact-finding and accounting capacities of police departments, administrative agencies, and courts of law. True, property rights are protected selectively rather than fairly for other, less palatable reasons as well. To the extent that publicly salaried officers devote more time to deterring and punishing acquisitive crimes in rich white neighborhoods than in poor black or Latino neighborhoods, property rights resemble the legally camouflaged interests of the strong. Such a lopsided enforcement of rights is surely a violation of equality before the law. But even if law enforcement officers did not favor some groups over others, they would still be selective in the delivery of protection from assault and theft.

Rights remain rights even though they will not always be enforced to the hilt, or even as thoroughly as would be possible were resources more plentiful or taxpayers more open-handed. Trade-offs in rights enforcement must and will be made. Scarce resources will be allocated between monitoring the police and (for example) paying and training the police, between monitoring the police and monitoring electoral officers, between monitoring the police and providing legal aid to the poor, providing food stamps to the poor, educating the young, nursing the elderly, financing national defense, or protecting the environment.

Morally speaking, incomplete protection of property rights is far easier to swallow than half-hearted protection of the helpless from beatings and killings. We accord property rights special, but not the greatest possible, protection. But are the interests of some Americans in not being brutalized or murdered given the same level of regard as the interests of other Americans in protection of their property rights? Was the palpable benefit to Joshua DeShaney of retaining his normal brain functions given the highest imaginable level of administrative protection? Was it accorded a level of protection greater or less than that received by the homeowners of Westhampton? There seems to be something obscene about the very comparison, not to mention the distressing answers such questions may elicit. But they do suggest that, in reality, *no* right can be uncompromisable, for rights enforcement, like everything costly, is inevitably incomplete.

Those who describe rights as absolutes make it impossible to ask an important factual question: Who decides at what level to fund which cluster of basic rights for whom? How fair, as well as how prudent, is our current system of allocating scarce resources among competing rights, including constitutional rights? And who exactly is empowered to make such allocative decisions? Attention to the costs of rights leads us not only into problems of budgetary calculation, as a consequence, but also into basic philosophical issues of distributive justice and democratic accountability. Indeed, it leads us to the edge of what is perhaps the outstanding philosophical dilemma of American political theory: What is the relationship between democracy and justice, between principles of collective decision-making, applicable to all important choices, and norms of fairness that we consider valid regardless of deliberative decisions or majority will?

In the *DeShaney* case, the Court was simply wrong to conclude that constitutional rights never include a right to state help. But it was right to the extent that it implicitly acknowledged a severe problem, for the protection of human lives always involves allocative decisions, and judges are not always in a good position to determine if one set of allocations is better or worse than the realistic alternatives. The cost of rights does not justify the Court's decision in the *DeShaney* case itself. More generally, however, scarcity is an entirely legitimate reason for the government's failure to protect rights absolutely. This insight draws out the commonalities between the first, second, and third generations of rights. All depend on collective contributions. All can be seen as selective investments of scarce resources. All are in an important sense aspirational, for none can ever be perfectly or completely enforced. Of course, there are differences as well. But the similarities are strong enough to belie the view that those rights that have been proposed and introduced more recently betray the basic spirit of the American Constitution.

PART III:

WHY RIGHTS ENTAIL
RESPONSIBILITIES

Chapter Nine
HAVE RIGHTS GONE TOO FAR?

WHILE STILL A HIGH SCHOOL STUDENT IN WISCONSIN, and only a minor, John Redhail became a father. The child's mother filed a successful paternity action against him, and the court ordered Redhail to pay $109 per month until the child reached the age of eighteen. Indigent and unemployed, Redhail did not make the payments. Two years later his application to marry Mary Zablocki was denied on the grounds that Redhail had failed to pay child support and, under Wisconsin law at the time, those who had not met their child support obligations could be deprived of the right to marry.

The Supreme Court of the United States held that the Wisconsin law in question was unconstitutional.[1] The right to marry, the Court explained, is "fundamental," and a state cannot enforce a support order through the unusual means of denying marriage licenses. Such license denials do not deliver money into any child's hands, and other available collection strategies would not intrude on constitutionally protected rights.

Should a deadbeat father's right to marry trump his moral responsibilities toward his child? This fundamental liberty obviously could not exist in the absence of governmentally created and managed procedures. In its current form, it is a product of government, not of nature. Should it not be abridged when doing so can "send a message" and perhaps help ensure that men fulfill their most basic social duty? Since the community defrays the costs whenever children become public charges, can it not restrict the freedom of those who are morally and legally obliged to provide support? Do private rights, when interpreted as preemptory claims, operate as excuses for moral shirking? Must our responsibilities to family and community wither and fade as the domain of our individual liberties expands?

Beneath these legal questions lurk even deeper worries. Has America recently witnessed an explosion of rights at the expense of traditional moral duties? Does our political culture now entice individuals to act however they please, without heeding the consequences, especially the consequences for others? Should it be obligatory for Americans—John Redhail and those in similar positions—to forgo their ephemeral and egotistical wants, pull up their socks, and act responsibly? And what is the relevance of the fact that private rights, such as those asserted by John Redhail, have public costs?

The idea that rights have "gone too far" while responsibilities have correspondingly shriveled has become something of a platitude. In the 1950s, according to a familiar tale, Americans enjoyed fewer rights, insisted much less on their personal freedoms, and (it supposedly follows) took their responsibilities to both self and others most earnestly. Since the 1960s, by glaring contrast, licentiousness has swept the land. Americans now think that it is a glorious idea to do whatever they have a right to do—to receive a paycheck while refusing to work, to abuse drugs and alcohol, to behave promiscuously, or to have children out of wedlock. Nor does this fable neglect the government's noxious role in promoting cultural decay. After the Supreme Court under Chief Justice Earl Warren and other government agencies started lavishing rights on nonconformists, ordinary citizens began to disregard their traditional duties. The government's irresponsible overprotection of rights helped breed the population's irresponsible neglect of obligations.

Claims to this effect issue from a dazzling variety of sources: President Clinton, Robert Dole, Supreme Court Justice Clarence Thomas, General Colin Powell, George Will, many members of the U.S. Senate, and a wide range of academics, including Mary Ann Glendon, Amitai Etzioni, William Galston, and Gertrude Himmelfarb. Glendon fears that "rights talk" has drawn Americans into greater selfishness and atomism, that a culture of rights has politically devalued altruism, mutual concern, and assistance to one another.[2] Will, Galston, and Powell plead for a resurrection of "shame" as a means of inculcating sobriety and discipline. Himmelfarb speaks of the "demoralization of society," meaning a wholesale retreat of morality from our social world, and draws unflattering comparisons between a degenerate America today and Victorian England, where pervasive respect for moral virtues purportedly ensured a greater role for social responsibility. Many critics complain that during the 1960s and 1970s the U.S. Supreme Court was seized by the promiscuous counterculture. Thereafter, it lavished rights unstintingly on the rebellious, the untrustworthy, and the deviant. This, they say, is how America began its current downward slide.

The notion that rights are intrinsically corrosive of duties is especially appealing to conservative critics of social programs designed to help the poor. But such apprehensions are also shared by liberals. Both ends of the current political spectrum identify rights with irresponsibility and an attenuated sense of duty, although they have different forms of moral laxity in mind. The Right belabors the licentiousness of the poor, while the Left laments the licentiousness of the rich. Conservatives typically decry the wanton behavior of young uneducated black mothers hooked on public aid. They claim that welfare entitlements undercut responsibility by delivering paychecks to those who refuse to get out of bed in the morning, dress themselves, and show up punctually for work. For their part, liberals deplore the reckless conduct of junk-bond dealers, overpaid CEOs, industrial polluters, and companies that relocate for a small profit regardless of how plant closings affect aging workforces and abandoned communities. They accuse the privileged of displaying a devil-take-the-hindmost fondness for their own property and privileges. One side is obsessed by the want of responsibility toward oneself, while the other focuses its outrage on irresponsibility toward others. But both aspire to restrict the liberties of those who fail to comply with basic moral rules. In this sense, John Redhail—brassily asserting his rights while furtively ducking his responsibilities—epitomizes what each camp believes to have gone wrong with America.

But is the United States today really suffering from a culture of "anything goes"? Do most Americans inconsiderately pursue immediate interests or impulses with little thought for social consequences? And can this cult of heedlessness, assuming it exists, be causally traced to an "explosion of rights"? In what sense, if at all, has the entitlement mentality caused family breakdown, sexual permissiveness, and a wasting of the work ethic? We are frequently asked to believe that individuals throughout the land have been shedding their responsibilities while scrambling greedily for their rights and that morality has been rinsed out of law. Since rights are ultimately latitudes or exemptions from control, we are told, irresponsible behavior is programmed into the genetic code of America's rights-based regime. In this view, after rights to get divorced and live off welfare began to be accepted without embarrassment in the United States, the country's citizens started thinking that there is nothing—however selfish or self-destructive or antisocial—that they are not licensed to do. To arrest the ongoing social decay, Americans of all classes must be weaned from their pathological attachment to personal liberties.

RESPONSIBILITY TALK

We should think more responsibly about responsibility. Have increases in criminal behavior resulted from the enforcement of rights or from, say, demographic, technological, economic, educational, and cultural changes largely independent of rights? Even if certain rights have, on balance, increased irresponsible behavior in some domains, sweeping causal generalizations are dubious. "Responsible behavior" may be defined as conduct that reduces harm to both self and others. Can we plausibly claim that there has been a general reorientation of American society from responsibilities (thus understood) to rights?

In many spheres of social life today, people shirk their duties, behave inconsiderately, ignore the serious problems of others, and ought, in general, to behave more responsibly. But this is no innovation of the last thirty years; in one form or another, it has always been the case. It is true today even in countries where individual rights are uniformly disrespected or wholly unknown. So what has the culture of rights added to mankind's enduring proclivity to recklessness, insensitivity, and short-term thinking?

Two possibilities have already been discussed at length. When interpreted either as negative immunities from government influence or as non-negotiable claims, rights may indeed become formulas for irresponsibility. If property owners are persuaded that their ownership rights are perfectly secured when their government simply steps out of the picture, they may also underestimate how thoroughly their individual freedoms depend on community contributions. When civil libertarians style a small number of rights as absolute, they may neglect the distributional consequences of expending scarce resources on a limited set of what they have identified as the most urgent social interests. Those who believe that they have a right to engage in certain behavior may not understand that it is not right to do what they have a right to do. So, yes, where rights are poorly understood, they can encourage irresponsible conduct.

Nevertheless, rights and responsibilities can hardly be separated; they are correlative. The mutual dependence of rights and responsibilities, their essential inextricability, makes it implausible to say that responsibilities are being "ignored" because rights have "gone too far." Add to this the fact that rights are immensely heterogeneous. Is the right to engage in collective bargaining, on balance, de-responsibilizing? What about habeas corpus? The right to a fair trial? The right to self-defense? The right to vote? Rights to due process and equal treatment do not tell government officials, at least, that "anything goes."

Ordinary contract law prohibits American courts from enforcing irresponsible debts, such as those contracted among gamblers. Such interdictions are natural, for contract law as a whole is a system for enforcing social responsibilities. The right

of a promisee to sue a promisor for breach of promise is the classical illustration of the thesis that rights and duties are correlative.[3] And the pattern is general. If Smith has a right to his
property, then Jones has a duty not to trespass upon it. If Jones
has a right to a percentage of the proceeds from his bestseller, the
publisher has a duty to send him what he is due. To protect the
rights of Smith the nonsmoker, the government must increase
the responsibilities of Jones the smoker. If Jones's freedom of
religion is constitutionally protected, public officials have
toward him a duty of toleration. If Smith has a right to be free
from racial discrimination in employment, employers have a
duty to ignore the color of Smith's skin. If Jones has a right in a
criminal trial to exclude evidence gathered illegally against him,
the police have a duty to get a valid warrant before they search
his house. If Smith has a right to sue a newspaper for libel, the
newspaper has a duty to check its facts.

The United States once denied enslaved African Americans
the rights to own property and to make contracts, to take care
of their children and to vote. These denials did not inculcate
habits of responsibility. Societies where liberal rights are weak-
ly enforced—that is, where predatory behavior among strangers
abounds—do not witness a flourishing of social responsibility.
Historical evidence suggests, on the contrary, that rightslessness
is the richest possible breeding ground for individual and social
irresponsibility. In this more sociological sense, too, rights and
responsibilities are far from opposites.

Contrary to the critique of those who seek more responsibility, the current American legal system, rather than reflecting the
anarcho-libertarian principle of "anything goes," publicly artic-
ulates and coercively enforces reams of legal prohibitions. And

many of these coercive constraints were created in the supposedly responsibility-phobic 1960s and 1970s—including rules against environmental degradation, against dangerous workplaces, and against the sexual harassment of working women. Some important constraints are much older, such as rules against unlicensed amateurs setting themselves up in private practice as eye surgeons. Today, the national government limits the right of tobacco companies to advertise their products on the grounds that such otherwise protected commercial speech decreases responsible behavior among the young. (Addiction means precisely this: addicted individuals cannot, in any simple sense, "freely choose" not to smoke; as a consequence, the government cannot foster individual liberty, where addictive substances are concerned, simply by assuming a posture of laissez-faire.) Social responsibility is far from neglected by American law. While amply supported by colorful anecdotes, the report of an across-the-board decrease in the social responsibility of Americans since the 1960s is scantily corroborated by reliable evidence.

Rights and responsibilities are routinely reconfigured as time passes; individuals now act responsibly in realms where they once behaved irresponsibly and vice versa. In some cases, at least, they have relinquished rights they once enjoyed. Here are a few examples:

- Social norms, and sometimes law, now discourage environmentally destructive behavior. In many circles, littering invites social disapproval. Recycling is common; people willingly recycle. Companies engage in a wide range of activities designed to reduce pollution, presumably to escape social disapproval and to act responsibly. One of the most effective environmental programs simply requires companies to make available to the public information about their toxic releases. Responding to public pressure, companies have substantially reduced their emissions. A more trivial but in its way remarkable example: In big cities, people clean up after their dogs.

- In general smoking has declined. From 1978 to 1990, a steep drop in cigarette smoking took place. The decline was especially pronounced among young African Americans, who have been exercising responsibility where they once indulged their liberties. The smoking rate among blacks between the ages of 18 and 24 fell from 37.1 percent in 1965, to 31.8 percent in 1979, to 20.4 percent in 1987, to 11.8 percent in 1991, to 4.4 percent in 1993. (There has been a disappointing rise since that time, but rates remain low by earlier standards.) Part of the decline stems from the fact that smokers no longer enjoy the legal rights they once took for granted: in many places, smoking is now illegal. Part of the drop-off also reflects a growing perception that smoking is harmful to both self and others.

- Whereas employers could once fire employees at will, they no longer have this right, at least not in its 1950s form. As a result of the Occupational Safety and Health Act, civil rights laws, workers' compensation laws in their modern guise, and common law developments, employers are now constrained in their authority to dismiss employees. Employers now labor under a legal duty to provide a safe workplace, and they can no longer discharge employees on discriminatory grounds. Social norms also discourage irresponsible (which is to say arbitrary) discharges.

- Employers and teachers were once free to engage in sexual harassment. Indeed, the very category of "sexual harassment" did not exist until recently, and both social norms and law authorized teachers and employers to seek sexual favors from those over whom they exercised power. Employers and teachers were essentially licensed to indulge in what is now punishable as harassing behavior. A traditional right has therefore been legally extinguished. Responsible behavior in this area is increasingly widespread, partly because of new law, and partly because of patterns of social disapproval that are inducing men to behave more responsibly.
- In many states, men no longer have a legal right to rape their wives. As a result of new legislation, husbands must act more responsibly. Sexual intercourse must be consensual even within marriage.
- Until recently, racist and anti-Semitic statements were common fare even in relatively public places. Such statements are still largely uncontrolled by law, and bigots have a legal right to utter racial slurs if they are so inclined. But many Americans shun talking in such irresponsible ways or at least do so less often than they once did. On this count, at least, civility has increased.

Even though socially and personally responsible behavior has fallen off in some areas, in other words, talk of a wholesale decline of responsibility is overblown. Indeed, it would not be especially difficult to concoct a self-congratulatory report on a whole new wave of responsibility in America: whereas they used to cling pertinaciously to their selfish rights, it could be said, Americans have now learned to act with generosity, social conscience, and concern for others. But why answer one half-baked narrative with another? What has happened in the last twenty years is a perfectly ordinary process of legal evolution, in which both responsibilities and rights have been redefined. The law has recognized some new rights while disestablishing some old ones.

Whether all of the recent developments are welcome is entirely beside the point. This kind of modification is only to be expected. In the relevant period both law and social norms have changed, as they never cease to do. Who knows what kinds of responsibilities and irresponsibilities will be produced by new law and new norms thirty years from now?

The dichotomy between rights and responsibilities is especially misleading because many rights are specifically created in order to make government more responsible. The right to exclude testimony extracted under duress is designed to prevent arresting and interrogating officers from beating confessions out of detainees. Most constitutional rights, in fact, are crafted to induce responsible conduct among agents of the state. They are incentives to self-discipline, partly but not only because rights imply duties. The right to vote and freedom of the press, especially, are meant to have, and sometimes do have, a responsibilizing effect on officials who can be ousted from office or held up to public ridicule.

When American law enforces social responsibility, it does not ordinarily do so in the name of an ideal code of conduct. Instead, American law usually imposes responsibilities as the counterparts, or preconditions, of rights. The responsibilities of polluters are the mirror image of the rights of the public to a nontoxic environment. Smokers and employers have duties because nonsmokers and employees have rights. The crime of marital rape, quite obviously, imposes a duty in the name of a right. The rights of stockholders are the duties of company directors and managers.

For a debtor to respect the rights of his creditor, he must act responsibly. So must a government that respects the contractually attained rights of all parties subject to its jurisdiction. Property rights inhibit both private theft and the confiscatory whims of public officials, thereby making both ordinary citizens and public officials behave more responsibly than they might otherwise tend to do. A government that enforces and protects rights, moreover, cannot do so unless it channels scarce tax revenues to public uses, rather than into the pockets of corrupt officials. Full and fair compensation for any property seized for public purposes requires a well-functioning system of public finance. The simple fact that rights have costs, therefore, already demonstrates why rights entail responsibilities.

Indeed, the cost of rights allows us to slip into the rights/responsibilities debate by a side door. Property rights have costs because, to protect them, the government must hire police officers. Responsibility is involved here, first, in the honest routing of taxpayers' dollars into the salaries of the police. It is involved a second time when, at considerable expense, the government trains police officers to respect the rights of suspects. And responsibility comes in a third time when the government, again at the taxpayers' expense, monitors police behavior and disciplines abuses to prevent officers from abridging civil rights and civil liberties by, for example, breaking into people's homes, manufacturing evidence, and beating up suspects. Attention to the cost of rights, in other words, heightens our understanding of the mutually supportive relationship between rights and responsibilities. And the same holds true when we turn from classical rights to the rights characteristic of the modern regulatory state.

The "social disintegration" litany of Left and Right will no doubt remain a staple of American political debates, for it apparently serves subcognitive needs. At least, laments of this sort cannot be easily quieted by evidence or argument. But such complaints are based on a serious misconceptualization of rights, and showing this may still be useful.

MORALITY IN LAW

American law, admittedly, vests individuals with the right to do things that are widely considered to be morally wrong. This is not an accidental but an essential feature of any liberal regime or indeed of any free country. Americans have the legal right to engage in conduct that responsible and even moderately sane people will scrupulously avoid. So while American law has moral sources, it is not coextensive with the moral sensibility of the community.

The indifference of law to morality, however, should not be exaggerated. The moral codes that impinge on law have changed somewhat, it is true, but they have not vanished, and it is not even clear that they have been reduced on balance. American tort law, for instance, remains shot through with morally laden categories such as "negligence" and "recklessness," and these categories routinely guide the way state power is used. In the past few decades, morally charged legal constraints on harmful behavior have increased, not decreased, in such areas as product liability and consumer protection. In criminal law, the perception that the accused has acted with "an abandoned and malignant heart" or "a culpable state of mind" continues to influence the decisions of prosecutors and judges alike. And in the United States, unlike in other Western countries, anyone who causes a death, however accidentally, while committing a felony, may be charged with murder—a perhaps futile attempt to make felons behave more responsibly while committing their lesser crimes.

Along the same lines, the list of crimes against morality that are still punished in America is quite impressive: statutory rape, incest, indecent exposure, prostitution, child pornography, and lewd and lascivious conduct.[4] Habitual drunkenness provides grounds for divorce in most states. Adultery remains illegal under the law of many states, as well as under American military law. And American law recognizes morality in another sense as well: to write or say that a person is immoral—that he is a womanizer or watches filthy movies or is a miser or would commit crimes if he were not afraid of getting caught—all this is, in some states, actionable per se and does not require the plaintiff to prove special damages. In other words, morality has hardly disappeared from our courtrooms or our streets.

Responsibility, moreover, is frequently a product of law. The right to drive a car does not include a right to drive it irresponsibly. In fact, since 1960 the law has imposed more, rather than fewer, constraints on both manufacturers and drivers, designed to increase safety. Spouses are still legally responsible for one another's debts. In most states, it remains very difficult to disinherit a spouse. Americans are also remarkably compliant with the tax laws (well over 90 percent of the public complies fully); indeed, Americans are far more compliant than citizens in some countries where individualism and individual rights play a less conspicuous role in social self-understanding. Massive tax evasion in, say, Russia today does not stem from a culturally ingrained attachment to individual rights. Yet observable increases in responsibility do not result only from fear of criminal and civil sanctions: without some element of "civic virtue," bolstered no doubt by the public perception that the government spends tax revenues more or less responsibly, that most people do their fair share, and that rich Americans, in particular, are not wholly exempt from taxation, the costs of running the Internal Revenue Service would be much steeper.

RIGHTS AS LATENT RESPONSIBILITIES

An accused party has a right to get out of jail on (not excessive) bail before trial in order to prepare a better defense. In this case, the rightsholder himself has a right to act responsibly. Not only do rights typically entail responsibilities for others vis-à-vis rightsholders, but rightsholders themselves are sometimes made more responsible by virtue of exercising their rights. This is another reason why the clarion call for fewer rights and more responsibilities is ultimately incoherent.

Aristotle objected to Plato's enthusiasm for collective child-rearing on the grounds that if everyone is responsible for every child, and if particular individuals are not denominated "parents," children will not receive decent care. The very same logic justifies the right to private property. If everyone owns everything then, in a sense, no one owns anything. One of the problems with this sad state of affairs is that in a system of collective ownership, the costs of dilapidation are spread thinly, and thus catastrophically, across society. Each individual in a position to maintain and repair property loses little by decay and gains next to nothing by maintenance. In a system without private ownership or coercive organization, the costs of maintenance are borne by each person, while the benefits of maintenance are widely shared. Hence individuals have scant incentive to engage in timely and arduous repairs. If rewards for upkeep and improvement cannot be captured by owners, houses and farms and factories are very unlikely to be kept up and improved. Acting with an eye to tomorrow, individuals deprived of enforceable property rights are likely to engage in uncoordinated inaction, or acts of negligence that produce massive collective harms. As Aristotle objected to Plato, private rights can be a spur to action that is socially beneficial and, from society's point of view, highly responsible.

Any farmer toiling to repay a bank loan can explain that the right to private property is both an onerous burden and an incitement to effort. Not only do property rights compel owners to pay the costs of their own property's dilapidation, but well-defined and unambiguously assigned property rights nourish responsibility by allowing individuals to capture the returns on their investments. They also help lengthen the time horizon of owners, who can thereby hope to benefit tomorrow from exertions made today.

Property rights also play an essential role in systems of political accountability, giving taxpayers a material incentive to monitor the way governments put reluctantly shelled-out tax revenues to use. So multiple linkages between private ownership and social responsibility are clear even before we look at the ways the American legal system uses rights to layer social responsibilities on top of ownership rights—imposing zoning restrictions on the sale of pornography, using the tax code to prod homeowners to safeguard and improve their assets, preventing factory owners and landowners from polluting the aquifers, and discouraging restaurant owners from shutting their doors to racial minorities.

Pleas to downplay rights and inculcate responsibilities are less helpful than their authors intend because they convey the impression that rights-and-responsibilities is a zero-sum game: any increase in one automatically decreases the other. They obscure the essential fact that, in the American legal system, rights are public services that the government must answerably deliver in exchange for tax revenues responsibly paid by ordinary citizens. Rights would go miserably unprotected if these mutual accountabilities failed. The exchange of equal rights for social cooperation lies at the heart of liberal-democratic politics. Rights are what responsive government and informed citizenship are all about. That rights have costs demonstrates their dependence on what we might as well call "civic virtue." Americans possess rights only to the extent that, on the whole, they behave as responsible citizens.

None of this is meant to deny the urgency of various issues touched upon by the advocates of "more responsibility." But drug use, AIDS, divorce, out-of-wedlock births, welfare as a way of life, single-parent families, children in poverty, and violent crime cannot be so casually traced to an alleged "culture of rights." The terrible social pathology of our public housing projects should be addressed in more concrete and less exalted terms. None of these problems can be solved by diminishing the respect for rights in American legal culture. Nor are useful solutions likely to arise from sweeping claims about the acids of modernity.

Chapter Ten
THE UNSELFISHNESS OF RIGHTS

POLITICAL THEORY KNOWS OF RIGHTS WITHOUT RESPONSIBILITIES, namely the pre-legal rights of individuals in philosopher Thomas Hobbes's "state of nature," where individuals have "even a right to one another's body."[1] To protect this sort of "right," though we should probably not call it that, every individual is a freelancer, forced to shift for himself. Truculent males are more likely than females to succeed at such a brutal game. To escape the state of nature means to obtain a wholly new kind of interest: a legal right, that is, a claim that carries with it serious responsibilities. All legally enforceable rights are "artificial" in the sense that they presuppose the existence of that imposing human artifice, the public power, designed to promote social cooperation and inhibit mutual harm.

To enjoy such rights, an individual must renounce his "natural right" to punish unilaterally all those who, in his subjective opinion, have injured him. This renunciation is the germ of liberal responsibility. That legally enforceable rights entail responsibilities, even in the rightsholder himself, is also apparent from the difference between seeking a remedy at law and paying a Mafia hit man to wreak private revenge. Indeed, the right to litigate, even if grossly overused, helps induce those whose interests have been grievously harmed to seek redress "responsibly," that is, within legal channels, rather than in vigilante fashion. When an injured party seeks remedy in court (instead of the back alley), she must make an effort to prove her case. To obtain a writ of sequestration or an order to garnish a debtor's wages, a creditor must bear a considerable burden of proof and face rebuttal in an open procedure. That is, the rights-holder herself must behave responsibly, in a public setting, if she wants government help in enforcing her claim.

When they work well, liberal rights shrewdly deploy incentives to induce responsible behavior and self-discipline among private citizens as well as among public officials.[2] One individual's rights to sue another for plagiarism, abuse of trademark, or commercial fraud—all of which entail a taxpayer-subsidized right of access to a public system of litigation—probably make people act on balance more "responsibly" (however that elusive term is defined) than they otherwise would. To inhibit irresponsible speech, the state provides a forum for vindicating interests in reputation. Legislators jack up damages to make sure homeowners responsibly shovel their sidewalks. And so forth.

Admittedly, my right to sue you for negligent behavior can be used frivolously or irresponsibly. But so can my right to vote or, for that matter, a bottle of tranquilizers. Because they place a legal power over others into the hands of individuals, legal rights can always be abused. The personal ordeal of being sued in court includes the costs of defending oneself at trial and of submitting to the disagreeable burdens of discovery. But to safeguard against a misuse of the power to bring an action for damages, liberal systems do not abolish the power (a cure worse than the disease), but instead create countervailing powers, by establishing, for instance, rules that throw financial hardship upon parties who lodge insubstantial or frivolous or fraudulent claims. These rules themselves take the form of rights—rights to be free from abuse of judicial process—which embed in American law a standard of responsible behavior.

The costs of rights include the cost of imposing sanctions for noncompliance. This explains why societies where rights are systematically ignored are anything but preserves of moral responsibility. Rights enforcement means that a politically organized society consistently and fairly punishes those who trample lawlessly upon the most important interests of others. To inhibit the abusive behavior of those who stand to gain from violating rights is impossible without dipping into public funds. Remedies for past rights violations and disincentives for future rights violations are costly because they always involve enforced responsibilities. The debtor must repay. The promisor must perform. And the judges who enforce contracts and punish lawbreakers must abstain from taking bribes.

As systems of incentives inducing self-limiting—and that means responsible—behavior, rights should be associated not with a hands-off but with a liberal, as opposed to authoritarian, regulatory style. Rights, from this perspective, should be described neither as latitudes nor as entitlements, but rather as consciously designed or historically evolved techniques for inducing sober, decent, and mutually respectful behavior. Rights compel both those who can exercise them and those who must respect them to internalize the harms that may result from their own laxities and misbehaviors.

Some theorists draw a historical distinction between individual rights, purportedly invented in modern times, and a "right order," allegedly embraced in antiquity and the Middle Ages (when "right conduct" supposedly flourished).[3] But the contrast is misleading. Historically, no such age of untrammeled civic virtue and responsibility ever existed. And liberal rights are today integral to our conception of a "right order." They encourage right conduct. While the results are certainly imperfect, and sometimes worse than that, rights in America have helped build a social constellation in which private individuals usually refrain from harming one another and where citizens more or less responsibly contribute to the Treasury while officials use these funds more or less responsibly to defray the costs of rights. This is probably the only sort of order possible in a large, heterogeneous society such as the United States, where people from widely different backgrounds and with diverse beliefs are asked to cooperate in a common life.

Because rights are costly, they could never be protected or enforced if citizens, on average, were not responsible enough to pay their taxes and public officials were not, on the whole, responsible enough to use extracted revenues for public purposes rather than pocketing them for private enrichment. The sad tale of America's decaying social fabric and failing civic virtues would be more persuasive, and the situation of the country more desperate, if citizens routinely refused to pay their taxes. One reason they do not resist more universally is that, by and large, their rights are enforced. That is to say, they see that their taxes are used at least in part to protect what they understand to be their basic liberties.

THE ENTITLEMENT MENTALITY?

Since rights and responsibilities, far from being mutually exclusive, are corollaries, to depict the evolution of the American rights culture as a dramatic eclipse of dutifulness by libertinage is to make a hash of social and legal reality. For the culture of rights is always also a culture of responsibility. Legal permissions logically imply legal obligations, and rights always restrict even as they permit. Formulated differently, to make the enforcement of rights into the principal goal of public policy, the United States has developed a regulatory style that necessarily emphasizes duties, prohibitions, obligations, and restraints. To potential violators, every right "just says no."

Even where there has been a perceptible decline in social responsibility, it is intellectually irresponsible to trace this downward slide to the growing appeal of individual rights. To be sure, people may well be engaging in more irresponsible sexual behavior than they did, say, in 1955. But this is itself a crude thought (are sexual harassment and marital rape, both newly against the law, responsible?), and in what sense has this trend been unleashed or accelerated by an expansion of legal rights? Are not levels of promiscuity far better understood as a product of changing social norms and technologies? Not only does evidence suggest that new contraceptive options have been an important contributor, but changing sexual mores reflect changing relations between men and women. One of the roots of the "sexual revolution" is the refusal of women to be held to different standards than men. Was American society more responsible when male promiscuity was admired and female promiscuity reviled? Once the playing field was leveled, so to speak, traditional prohibitions and inhibitions began to crumble. Explaining why such moral norms and social expectations change when they do is far from easy. But there were undoubtedly multiple causal factors at work, the massive entry of women into the workforce and the greater availability of contraception being two. It would certainly be adventurous to suppose that the lengthening list of legally recognized rights was the principal moving force.

But what about the commonplace that a "right to welfare" discourages productive labor? This sounds rather plausible at first hearing. But an argument on the other side, formulated by Adam Smith, also has a certain weight: "That men in general should work better when they are ill fed than when they are well fed, when they are disheartened than when they are in good spirits, when they are frequently sick than when they are generally in good health, seems not very probable."[4]

Even if we accept Smith's speculations, should we not be worried by the growth of the entitlement mentality? Has not the overextension of welfare rights encouraged dependency, unwanted children, or other social ills? Can we not encourage responsible conduct by cutting back on public aid? These are legitimate questions, and there is some evidence that welfare rights have produced dependency and associated social ills. But the data are mixed.[5] This is especially true of the claim that rising illegitimacy rates are a product of public largesse. Evidence collected on the most important (and now repealed) welfare program, Aid to Families with Dependent Children (AFDC), does not unambiguously demonstrate that welfare fosters illegitimacy. Under the AFDC program, welfare rates were actually decreasing in the period when illegitimacy rates were increasing. Reductions in AFDC benefits do not correlate with decreases in illegitimate births, and increases in AFDC benefits do not correlate with increases in illegitimate births. Thus the data create a serious question of interpretation.

Food stamps may lessen the ordeal of being poor, and whenever it becomes especially horrible to be poor, fewer people may be poor, but this does not by itself demonstrate that food stamps breed sloth or multiply illegitimate births. A great deal depends on prevailing social norms associated with work, welfare, and family. In many sectors of society, these norms powerfully encourage steady employment, stigmatize public aid, and condemn out-of-wedlock pregnancy. When such norms lose their sway over hearts and minds, it is difficult to determine the precise extent to which welfare rights play a supplementary role in discouraging work or increasing rates of childbirth among poor unmarried women. As a result, it is far from obvious that penalizing single mothers financially will substantially reduce the frequency of single motherhood. To say so is not to defend existing welfare programs; whatever the shortcomings of such programs, the blanket claim that rights breed irresponsibility simply should be greeted with skepticism and tested by evidence.

THE QUESTION OF SELFISHNESS

A prominent and especially evenhanded critic of rights, Professor Mary Ann Glendon echoes widespread worries about the way rights undermine responsibilities and political culture in general. "Our current American rights talk," she claims, stands out for "its prodigality in bestowing the rights label, its legalistic character, its exaggerated absoluteness, its hyperindividualism, its insularity, and its silence with respect to personal, civic, and collective responsibilities."[6] With this alleged lopsidedness of our legal culture in mind, Glendon devotes considerable attention to the "duty to rescue," a duty not recognized by American law. If a bystander ignores someone who is drowning, he will not be held accountable, even if the rescue could have been accomplished with little effort. Glendon deplores this result, arguing at a minimum for a statement, in law, that such a duty exists. Such a duty might initially seem to be far removed from the legalistic world of individual rights. But appearances can be misleading. Implicitly, Glendon's argument for a new duty is a plea for a new right: a right to assistance, to be granted to vulnerable people and held by them against other individuals and the government. With a similar logic, antiabortion activists aim to discourage what they consider to be immoral and irresponsible behavior by creating a constitutional right to life and vesting it in the fetus. Not only do rights create duties, but the imposition of a duty often serves to create a right.

The culture of rights is simultaneously a culture of liabilities and hence of responsibilities. So why should rights in general be accused of promoting selfishness? The right to vote gives public officials an incentive to put their self-interest to one side, or rather to identify their personal interest (in being re-elected) with the public's interest in good governance. The rights to equal protection and to fair hearings do not seem especially amoral or antisocial. The rights protected under the Fourteenth Amendment are aimed at eliminating the immoral and antisocial effects of racial discrimination by public officials within the states. Far from being antisocial, such rights promote communal decency by protecting against the exclusion of subordinated groups. Many rights reflect some degree of altruism on the part of ordinary citizens and most, when reliably protected, can help increase altruism and habits of responsibility.

Some of the core liberal rights—such as freedom of speech and association—are designed to encourage forms of deliberation and communal interaction, practices that the critics of "rights talk" otherwise seem to favor. Freedom of association conspicuously protects collective action. So does the right to preach or to put out a newspaper. These freedoms are meant to stimulate social communication, not to protect isolated individuals in a presocial order or to promote back-turning on others and hedonistic self-involvement. Although the right to freedom of speech may be owned and used by individuals, it is also the precondition of an eminently social process, namely, democratic deliberation. Free speech fosters liberal sociality, the opportunity for people to communicate and disagree and bargain freewheelingly with one other in public arenas. Freedom of the press, which props open public channels of communication, is emphatically communal in character. Indeed, anyone who owns a speech right may, by using it, conceivably contribute to the collectivity and its goals. This is why the government cannot "buy" speech rights, even if speakers privately wish to sell them.

The right to receive a jury trial and the right to serve on a jury (regardless of race) are two additional time-honored American liberties that are far from atomistic. In these cases, the community purchases a right that ensures an important role for ordinary citizens in adjudicative proceedings. To say that Americans live in a "procedural republic" is to acknowledge that individuals are not judges in their own cases and that citizens create and maintain (among other things) common institutions through which they can solve some of their common problems. Part of the goal of a fair trial is to ensure that diverse citizens can work together to decide accurately questions of guilt or innocence. The constitutional right to due process—like the private right to bring an action in contract or tort—presupposes that, at the taxpayers' expense, the government makes fact-finding institutions accessible to those whose interests are at stake. The right to a fair trial is eminently social. It provides an important mechanism for community self-governance.

As mentioned earlier, the rights created under contract law and tort law can be just as accurately described as legal powers. The right to sue for negligence or breach of contract implies the power to impose a severe, even debilitating, financial burden on another human being. Since our legal system creates and maintains such dangerous instrumentalities, which may occasionally be exploited for private advantage, it must also make an effort to ensure that they are wielded responsibly. It must provide relief from wrongful findings of liability and mistaken repossession. And this it does, although imperfectly. Irresponsible and frivolous suits are no doubt a curse, but the American legal system nevertheless devotes considerable resources to discouraging the misuse of well-protected rights, including the right to sue.

Blackstone put the case for the procedural republic this way: "if individuals were once allowed to use private force as a remedy for private injuries, all social justice must cease, the strong would give law to the weak, and every man would revert to a state of nature."[7] The culture of rights encourages people to settle their conflicts juridically, to seek redress for their grievances through legal channels, without resort to violence and threats of violence. This is no small contribution to peaceful social coexistence and cooperation.

Chapter Eleven
RIGHTS AS A RESPONSE TO MORAL BREAKDOWN

WE HAVE A RIGHT TO SPEAK OFFENSIVELY, even abhorrently, but most people do not and should not exercise this right very often. A lawyer has a right to refuse to do pro bono work, but lawyers should generally do pro bono work. An extremely wealthy person has a right to hoard all his money (after taxes) and to give none of it to charity, but miserliness is not to be encouraged. The right to make an enforceable will can be used by a multimillionaire lavishly to appoint his favorite cat cemetery, but he should support more deserving social causes.

Some Americans may think that, because they have a right to do something, they cannot be criticized or blamed for doing it. Some extremists, including broadcasters and Hollywood producers and owners of music companies, interpret any objection to their offensive or degrading talk as an unwarrantable violation of their freedom of speech. But a well-functioning liberal culture distinguishes legal sanction from moral censure.

Philosophers distinguish between "the right" and "the good," that is, between the uniform rules of justice Americans are jointly compelled by law to obey, and the various personal ideals they severally choose to embrace. In the same spirit, a distinction can be drawn between the legally wrong and the personally immoral. We avail ourselves of the public power to deter unlawful breaches of promise, torts, and crimes. To discourage behavior that is immoral but not illegal, by contrast, we deploy private persuasion and disapproval, but not public coercion.

Under the U.S. Constitution as currently interpreted, women have a right to have abortions. For many Americans, this right epitomizes the way individual liberty promotes personal irresponsibility. It is certainly inadequate to justify abortion simply by invoking the right to "privacy"—a word that does not appear in the Constitution and that, in any case, fails to do justice to the issue. To oppose the abstract "right to life" to the equally abstract "right to choose" is also of little help. Rather than protecting an abstract right to choose, we should probably be focusing on the most effective way to provide young women with decent opportunities and prospects. But lawful efforts to discourage pregnancies that are likely to result in abortions, and even to dissuade pregnant women from undergoing abortions, should not be uniformly banned as interferences with a "right." The right to abortion imposes correlative responsibilities on public officials, and some of these, such as police protection for employees at abortion clinics, require the expenditure of taxpayers' money. Nonviolent efforts to reduce the staggering number of abortions per year (a grim 1.5 million), at least if accompanied by affirmative help for those with few options, may well be excellent investments.

Law should be and is shaped by moral aspirations, and it is perfectly consistent, from a moral standpoint, to insist that the right to an abortion ought to be exercised, or should have to be exercised, only very rarely. Steps can be taken to make abortions less common, as through education about contraception, prevention of coercive intercourse, and better opportunities for young women.

However we may think about this vexing subject, it demonstrates that while individuals may have a perfect legal right to do something, others can have an equal right to complain nonviolently about their doing it. Indeed, a large part of moral education consists of the inculcation of norms and values that discourage behavior that is harmful or offensive but not unlawful. Behavior of questionable morality can be effectively discouraged by informal social opprobrium, without turning it into a crime or a tort.

According to some self-styled advocates of responsibility, a new emphasis on what people have a right to do has produced a culture of moral relativism and standardlessness in which Americans typically insist on their rights without giving a second thought to whether their conduct is valuable to themselves or society. These cultural critics are particularly worried that grants of rights lead people, and especially disadvantaged people, to think of themselves as victims, and to specialize in seeking redress and protection from government. The recognition of rights, they conclude, can fuel dependency, self-pity, and lack of initiative.

Similar worries about rampant "victimology" have recently surfaced in arguments about sex equality. Some critics of feminism—and some feminists—argue that an overemphasis on rights against sexual harassment, date rape, and pornography has abraded the sense of personal agency and responsibility and encouraged women to enroll in a cult of victimhood, thereby making it all the more difficult for them to obtain equality and self-respect. Admittedly, people who regard themselves as victims, who do not perceive their own capacities for self-help, and who think that the world somehow owes them a living may fail to engage in activity that is ultimately rewarding to themselves or society. But there is little historical evidence to support the speculation that people who gain legal rights uniformly begin to see themselves as passive victims who need assume no responsibility for their own fate. Everything depends on the particular legal rights in question, for those who enjoy particular rights often have more agency as a result.

Many critics of the regulatory-welfare states are enthusiastic about rights of contract and property and would like to strengthen the legal protection given to those rights by, for example, requiring government to compensate people whose land loses value as a result of government regulation. Such critics are asking, in effect, for new or strengthened rights. But would it be plausible to allege that stronger rights of property and contract would debase their beneficiaries into victims, or that people who urge such rights are promoters of "victimology"? This is an odd claim, even though rights of property and contract do erode certain archaic habits of self-help—even though those who purchase private security or fire prevention services are likely thereafter to refrain from honing their traditional capacities for self-defense.

In fact, people whose rights are reliably enforced—including their rights to make contracts, to own property, to be free from segregation, and to be free from sexual harassment—may also be likely to be more secure actors in society and to cooperate more actively with a system that grants them equal respect. Some rights are even a precondition for individual agency: individuals who lose control of their person and property become far more likely to see themselves as victims. Perhaps those who until now have been neglected by their government would stop playing "victim" and become agents and citizens if their rights were reliably protected. Indeed, a crucial social purpose of rights protection is to do precisely this. Whether rights increase or decrease self-reliance depends on their content, context, and effects. To suggest that rights as such reduce those who enjoy them into helpless supplicants and victims—replacing family with promiscuity and work with dependency—is not plausible.

Martin Luther King, Jr., called on the state for protection against private racial discrimination. As a litigator, Thurgood Marshall helped establish a right against racial discrimination by the state. Neither King nor Marshall can be plausibly accused of promoting a cult of victimhood. On the contrary, they are generally thought to have helped establish greater independence for African Americans. (King, incidentally, although often described as an enthusiast for racial neutrality and color-blindness, was a resolute supporter of race-conscious affirmative action programs.) Their advocacy of rights was part and parcel of their reformist dynamism and refusal to assume a passive stance.[1] What would someone who advocates responsibility while denegrating rights say about their assertion of rights? Would he really describe it as a fatal first step toward the cult of victimization among African-Americans?

RIGHTS ARISE WHERE NORMS AND DUTIES FAIL

So how, if at all, can the abortion right be best justified? The answer has everything to do with social context, not to mention with pervasive failures of social responsibility that extend far beyond the parties most immediately involved. Under conditions of equality on the basis of sex, the argument for a constitutionally protected abortion right in the United States would be far weaker. Without widespread poverty, the right to have an abortion within the United States—that is, the right to have an abortion without undertaking an expensive trip abroad—would raise less serious questions of basic fairness. In a society in which duties to the vulnerable were taken very seriously, the case for a right to an abortion would be less plausible than it now is. In such a society, women who need help would get it—before, during, and after pregnancy. The availability of social assistance would argue against the right to abortion, by making child-bearing and child-rearing less difficult and less a source of inequality than they now are for many women. In such a society, men as well as women would be required (by social norms, if not by law) to dedicate their bodies to the protection of their children. (It is noteworthy that nowhere in American law are men required to devote their bodies to the protection of third parties, even when their own children, for example, need a blood transfusion or a bone-marrow transplant.) Most important, in such a society, restrictions on abortion would be based on a general and neutral form of compassion for the vulnerable, rather than the now-pervasive desire—prominent, though by no means universal, in the pro-life movement—to control women's sexual and reproductive capacities.

In other words, abortion rights would be harder to justify if restrictions on abortion did not allow male legislators, administrators, and judges to impose traditional gender roles through law, and in that way to continue a system of discrimination based on sex. In a society free from sex discrimination, any right to abortion might seem puzzling or even unnecessary. But this is not the society in which Americans now live.

Under conditions of pervasive gender inequality, the protection of abortion rights can best be understood as a social answer, as responsible as any alternative in light of those conditions, to a tragic initial failure of social responsibility. The right to have an abortion is harder to justify in the abstract. Here lies a general lesson: rights often emerge when private and public institutions falter and individuals fail to carry out their duties responsibly. When the environment is severely degraded, when the vulnerable are abandoned to fend for themselves, or when children are at risk, "rights claims" are commonly raised. When individuals engage in criminal behavior because bad social conditions have loosened moral inhibitions (thou shalt not steal, thou shalt not kill), the costs of providing police protection are sharply increased, and new claims of rights arise from the victims of crime. Hence the proposed Victims' Rights Amendment to the Constitution is a response to both individual and social dereliction. The claims of rights to clean air and water, to food, to a decent place to live, to a safe workplace, to children's rights, or to "free reproductive choice"—all these must be understood in context as compensatory responses to an original dereliction of social responsibility.

When beneficial social norms are working well, legal regulations often prove unnecessary. When beneficial norms break down, rights claims become increasingly insistent. Social norms and legal rules solve similar problems by different means. A strong social norm against littering would have the same effect as a well-enforced law against littering. Both would help society avoid behavior that is in each case not terribly bothersome, but that is in the aggregate highly undesirable. Like laws, social norms help coordinate social behavior. To the extent that Americans live in the grip of norms of cooperation, which pervasive-ly encourage people to do their share by contributing small amounts of time or labor to projects that can succeed only when a large majority makes such contributions, rights claims do not even arise.

Informal social disapproval is often more powerful and effective than legal rules enforced by courts of law and can provide a less expensive and more efficient way to achieve widely desired social aims. If companies are polluting too much, if smokers are irritating or endangering nonsmokers, or if poor people are using drugs, public education campaigns to promote community norms might be able to improve the situation at a relatively low cost. Admittedly, the American government does not have a particularly sterling record as the moral preceptor of the nation. And preaching at people does not always make them good. (The audience may tune out or even rebel.) But government can and often does use the spread of information or the colorful depiction of the benefits of cooperation to society's advantage: increases in recycling and decreases in cigarette smoking are two recent examples.

When efforts at moral persuasion fail, rights are likely to be asserted instead. Arguments "against rights," therefore, may make more sense if reinterpreted as complaints about inadequate social norms and our need to respond to their defects. The right to be free from certain kinds of pollution ("nonsmokers' rights") and the right to be free from racial hate speech (a right vindicated by many campus speech codes) are regularly advanced when social norms falter. And once such rights are legally recognized, the costs to the taxpayer may be high.

Not all social norms are good; some are evil. A social norm against allowing black Americans to vote thwarted the purposes of the Fifteenth Amendment for almost a century. Indeed, the cost of rights enforcement is sometimes prohibitively high because pernicious social norms often cannot be broken without resorting to unconscionable force. The difficulty of enforcing civil rights in the teeth of racist habits and beliefs illustrates the point. The right to be protected from racial discrimination is better enforced in the United States military than in our civil society partly because civilians in the grip of racist norms have a greater capacity to resist the commands of authority than racists in uniform.

Rights enforcement is dependent both on coercive authority and on social norms, good or bad. It is limited because coercive authority is limited by scarce resources and because, whereas socially beneficial norms can make rights and coercion unnecessary, socially divisive norms can cripple them both or even render them futile. Legal rights may arise in response to faltering norms, but they will not be respected or enforced in the absence of at least some normative appeal. Prohibition—enacted as a kind of victims' rights amendment designed to protect the families of heavy drinkers—is probably the most vivid example. Likewise, such "welfare rights" as AFDC were ultimately doomed because they came to lack widespread public support.

None of this suggests that there has been a general shift in America away from responsibilities and toward rights. In 1995, despite the many John Redhails among us, more than ten billion child support dollars were collected in the United States,[2] a historic high. In countless other areas, too, people are now much more responsible than they used to be. And their enhanced responsibility often seems connected to a broadening and deepening of rights.

Yet when the state's capacity to protect its citizens is limited, it should be careful about mechanically enforcing moral responsibilities. As one commentator has recently remarked of coarse-grained legal attempts to compel deadbeat fathers to take responsibility for their children, "Poor mothers often break up with the father of their children because he is physically abusive. Once the break comes, they want him out of their lives. If a state agency forces an angry, abusive man to start paying child support, he may reassert his parental rights and begin harassing the mother again. Fanning these embers may not, in fact, be such a good policy."[3] If authorities drag a deadbeat father back into the life of his abandoned child, then they owe the child, and its mother, protection from the physical abuse that may ensue. A responsible government will not declare and enforce the rights of child support recipients if it is not prepared on the spot to pay the costs of such protection. The exercise of legal rights often invites a violent response and the cost of protecting rightsholders from retaliation should certainly be counted among the cost of rights themselves. No responsible political community will extend rights to its citizens unless it is willing to pay these subsidiary costs as well.

By their nature, in sum, rights impose responsibilities, just as responsibilities give birth to rights. To protect rights, a responsible state must responsibly expend resources collected from responsible citizens. Instead of lamenting a fictional sacrifice of responsibilities to rights, one should ask which concrete package of complementary rights and responsibilities is likely to confer the most benefits on the society that funds them.

PART IV:

UNDERSTANDING RIGHTS
AS BARGAINS

Chapter Twelve
HOW RELIGIOUS LIBERTY PROMOTES STABILITY

WHY DO AMERICANS OBEY THE LAW? Why do most U.S. citizens, most of the time, voluntarily adjust their behavior to intricate legal rules, pay their taxes, show up for jury duty, and go along with the occasionally unreasonable decisions of sundry political and judicial officials? A complete answer to "the compliance question" would no doubt allude to habit, imitation, deference, respect for norms, social solidarity, and the coercive power of the state. But ordinary citizens will not routinely respect the law if they do not also perceive it as legitimate. And that means they must see the burdens imposed by law as more or less fairly shared.

Compliance with law partly derives from a social understanding that the government safeguards and promotes fundamental human interests, including basic individual liberties. That is to say, the enforcement of rights not only presupposes the power to tax and spend, it also helps create popular acceptance of the power to tax and spend. Incumbents create political goodwill by funding rights that citizens want. While the protection of basic rights depends fundamentally upon the actions of the coercive and extractive state, the coercive and extractive activity of the state can be justified in the eyes of its citizens by its contribution to protecting, in an even-handed way, their most cherished interests.[1]

One reason why citizens feel morally obliged to fulfill elementary civic duties is that the system they thereby uphold adequately, though by no means perfectly, defends their fundamental freedoms. Legally and politically protected rights are among the most widely prized public services delivered by the liberal-democratic state. And American citizens willingly shoulder the not-inconsiderable burdens imposed upon them by their national, state, and local governments in part because these governments distribute with a modicum of fairness a whole range of precious public goods, such as firefighting and enforceable private rights. While the state musters protection, citizens reciprocate with cooperation. Cooperation is much less likely to be forthcoming when rights protection is diluted, erratic, or absent, or when government creates and protects rights that should not qualify as such. Incumbents also have a deplorable tendency to stint on the protections they offer to politically weak individuals and groups whose cooperation they do not especially need.

The rights-for-cooperation swap is a perennial theme of liberal political theory, usually evoked with the celebrated metaphor of a "social contract." The government agrees to protect citizens both from each other and from its own rogue officials; in exchange, citizens lend the government their support. Liberal societies are held together not only by habit, authority, shared culture, feelings of belonging, and fear of the police, but also by a widespread perception of mutual advantage. This is one reason why people feel reluctant to contribute their share if others are shirking. Societies flourish when individuals exercise mutual self-restraint, submit themselves to clear rules binding equally on all, and pull their weight in common endeavors. When these pieces are in place, individual burdens are perceived to be out-weighed by individual and collective gains.

An empirically oriented theory of rights must consider how individual liberties create and sustain cooperative relations both among groups of citizens and between citizens and their government.[2] Why should citizens willingly defray the costs of rights enforcement? They may disburse from fear, of course, or from habit, without asking why. But they may also perceive these rights to be worth the price. This is what it means to call rights and especially basic rights the cornerstone of the liberal social contract, the source of the legitimacy of liberal political authority. Granted by governments and accepted by citizens in a trading of concessions, rights may even, at a stretch, be deemed bargains. This is not the whole story, but it is a helpful metaphor. Indeed, it is more than metaphor; as a purely descriptive or historical matter, many rights owe their origin to bargains among diverse people seeking to cooperate or at least to coexist peaceably with one another.[3] By attempting to construe them in this way, we can clarify how rights can be regularly safeguarded by government action, even if they cannot, for practical reasons, always be enforced in courts of law.

Some of those who wince at the very mention of the cost of rights may distrust close inquiry into the trade-offs that rights enforcement inevitably entails. They may also object on moral or theoretical grounds to the notion that rights are granted in exchange for civil cooperation, of which tax "contributions" are but the most easily metered example. Neglect of the question of the cost of rights may reflect an even deeper discomfort with the conception of rights as bargains. If rights are unassailable and universal, based on impartial reason and claimable by all rational beings, how can they be reduced to a matter of "you scratch my back while I scratch yours"? And indeed this way of formulating the matter does seem crass and simple-minded. If many rights cannot be bought and sold on the marketplace of commodities—if you cannot sell your right to speak freely or your vote—how can we assimilate rights generally to items in a barter exchange?

The answer is that bargains come in different forms and many of them are neither petty nor ignominious. Mutually beneficial and perfectly honorable trades occur every day—in workplaces, families, and statehouses as well as in supermarkets—and they are not objectionable simply because they are perceived to be advantageous to everyone involved. For instance, to lower the intensity of industrial strife, which might well disrupt interstate commerce, the American government assigns some rights to employers and some rights to employees and then tries to enforce the assembled package of rights and duties against the parties. Rights enforcement, in this case, is actually a strategy of conflict management and a form of bargain enforcement. Indeed, the use of rights to enhance mutually beneficial social cooperation is perfectly routine, as the very idea of a social contract should suggest. Laws themselves, creating and embodying rights, are sometimes best understood as bargains. To say that rights can be seen as services delivered to fulfill the terms of a bargain is simply to affirm that rights-based political systems are stabilized in part—though only in part—by a widespread perception of mutual gain. By setting forth clear rules for resolving disputes without violence and stabilizing social expectations in a heterogeneous society, rights create a particularly stable style of social coexistence and cooperation.

As instruments for improving individual and collective welfare, rights naturally require renunciations of various kinds from all members of the community (not only from public officials), renunciations that ought to be abundantly repaid by the benefits that ensue from reciprocity, specialization, and the pooling of efforts. So the American social contract should not be described simply as a rights-for-cooperation exchange, with government serving up rights and citizens answering with cooperation. The American social contract involves a more deliberative and reflective deal among rights-respecting citizens themselves, between the rich and poor, for example, and among members of discordant religious sects.

Roughly speaking, theorists of democracy fall into two camps: those who see politics as a matter of interest-group deals among self-interested private groups and those who see politics as a process of deliberation and reason-giving. But dealing and deliberating both play roles in the creation of rights, and they are not easy to disentangle in practice. "Bargains" (or agreements) can and do emerge from processes of discussion and reflection, with self-interest, narrowly understood, not being the principal or only moving force. Indeed, social pacts codified into legally enforceable rights often reflect judgments about what is ultimately right and fair, not merely about what is convenient at the moment. But even when politics is dominated by deliberative democracy, so that narrow interests do not overwhelm the process of reason-giving, the quest for compromise and mutual adjustment often play a significant and even constructive role.

Religious liberty can be usefully examined along these lines. A classical liberal right with many abstract or philosophical rationales, freedom of conscience originated and evolved in large measure as a bargain among private social groups meant to ensure intersectarian comity, mutual forbearance, and social cooperation.

"CONGRESS SHALL MAKE NO LAW RESPECTING an establishment of religion, or prohibiting the free exercise thereof." These two rules have proved surprisingly difficult to reconcile. Conflicts between the free exercise clause and the no-establishment clause continue to raise some of the thorniest problems in American constitutional law. When protecting free exercise, by making civil halls available for religious meetings, does the state help establish a religion? When banning religious organizations from receiving generally available funds, does the state obstruct free exercise? Attempts to comply strictly with any interdiction of political support for religion—such as the ban on school-ordered prayer or the refusal to allow religious groups to use school facilities after hours—might be thought to place illicit burdens on free exercise. Similarly, scrupulous attempts to secure free exercise—by paying welfare benefits, for example, to those who refuse to accept employment because it would require them to work on the Sabbath—might seem to violate the prohibition on public support for private belief.

The practical dilemma here, whatever else it implies, reinforces one of the central claims of this book. Even those who seek neutrality about religion insist that the state must provide its standard services—above all police and fire protection—to religious organizations as well as to everyone else. This costs a great deal of money, especially when tensions among religious groups, or between the religious and the nonreligious, are running feverishly high. Because it regularly provides benefits to many nonreligious groups in society, the state cannot achieve a semblance of neutrality without subsidizing religion in numerous contexts. A government policy of hands off (no establishment) does not guarantee individual liberty (free exercise). Laissez-faire provides distinctly inadequate protection of the right to free exercise of religion. Advocates of school prayer must surely acknowledge as much. And those who reject school prayer, too, should be able to see that constitutional rights to free exercise of religion cannot be upheld by a state policy of noninterference, but instead require government performance and taxpayer support.

Yet the costs that religious liberty regularly impose upon taxpayers are poorly understood. One reason is that freedom of religion is routinely perceived as an exemplary "negative" liberty, designed to stay the government's hand, to curtail the power of Congress and state legislatures to interfere with the freedom of individuals to worship, believe, and live according to their consciences. In this conventional view, freedom of religion is designed to shut the government out of a walled-off private space in order to preserve the moral autonomy of individuals dealing with their hopes and fears about (among other things) their own and their loved ones' mortality.

In this context, the doctrine of non-entanglement and the image of a "wall of separation" between church and state are typically invoked to demonstrate that freedom of religion, like all other constitutional rights, requires the state to withdraw rather than to intrude, to refrain from acting rather than to act, to disengage rather than to engage. Freedom of religion, it is said, shelters vulnerable individuals—whether in solitary moments of prayerful reverie or unorthodox dissent or simple nonbelief—from the intrusive and conformist pressures of a potentially bigoted state.

Yet the contribution of religious liberty to individual autonomy should not be allowed to obscure its origin in, and contribution to, peaceable social coexistence. While permitting us to
be autonomous in our deepest convictions, religious liberty
depends essentially on the smooth functioning of a certain kind
of legitimate political authority. It also enables our religiously
heterogeneous society to operate passably well, playing a stabilizing role and encouraging social concert. Its obvious utility in
a religiously heterogeneous society helps account for the original
recognition of the right, for its enormous contemporary importance in America and elsewhere, and for the evident willingness of taxpayers to defray its costs.

Religious liberty is certainly no more costless than other
legal rights. American citizens are more or less free to worship or
not, as they wish, but their freedom in this respect makes a
claim upon the public fisc, even when it is not subsidized out
of public budgets (through, for example, police and fire protection of churches and other religious institutions). For instance,
religious liberty entitles citizens to judicial remedies (funded
by taxpayers) whenever religious freedoms are infringed by public officials. Although the law on this point is shifting and complex, religious liberty may on occasion require exemptions from
general law, and exemptions can prove expensive.[4]

Religious liberty is costly, to an even greater degree, because
it implies government readiness to intervene impartially whenever serious tensions arise among sects. Religious conflict in
America presents a legitimate arena for government regulation,
and therefore imposes all the ordinary public costs of monitoring, deterrence, and access to relief. Able to organize themselves
and express their views in public, Jehovah's Witnesses can play

anti-Catholic records in Catholic neighborhoods. Such freedom will certainly make claims upon the Treasury when, for example, it requires police supervision of potentially provocative expressions of religious fervor. Perhaps more pertinent today, religious liberty requires the government to supply relief if a private sect or church illicitly uses threats of coercion to prevent individual members from exit or apostasy.

Controversies continue to rage about the degree to which secular norms may be imposed on religious communities. Should antidiscrimination principles be applied against churches that, for example, discriminate on the basis of sex? In general American law answers that they should not be, although this answer has not gone uncontested. By contrast, the ban on ordinary civil wrongs—assault, battery, trespass, and so forth—is fully applied to religious organizations. However one judges the Court's 1990 decision to uphold the criminalization of peyote use in American Indian religious ceremonies (on the ground that the law was neutral and did not discriminate against religion),[5] freedom of religion in the United States would soon become illusory if religious cults operated freely behind a wall impenetrable to government officials, where no coercive public authority could be brought to bear, for example, on unscrupulous or mentally unhinged cult leaders. Because rights are potentially dangerous powers, a government committed to enforcing rights must also work to ensure that they are not seriously abused.

Religious liberty is tolerable only when it is practiced according to certain rules of civilized self-restraint, rules that must be coercively enforced. Religious groups in America are forbidden from using coercion or threats of coercion in pursuing their religious convictions, for the right to do so belongs exclusively to the government.[6] The government alone wields this right because it is, or claims to be, the only agent that represents the interests not of one sector, region, class, or sect in society, but rather the public interest, that is, the broadly shared interests of all citizens without exception, whatever their religious beliefs.

Superficial appearances aside, freedom of religion has nothing to do with state inaction or paralysis. It does not even imply that government must refrain from action (refrain, say, from enforcing laws against murder, or rape, or possessing hallucinogens) within the confines of church property. Rather than prohibiting state interference in sectarian affairs, the First Amendment simply regulates the manner and scope of such action. More profoundly, religious liberty provides a script for publicly subsidized cooperation and mutuality. It stipulates, for example, that citizens in a multidenominational America, when acting through the shared instrumentalities of their government, cannot publicly proclaim that adherents of minority sects and nonbelievers are second-class citizens or somehow unworthy or unwelcome members of the community.

The phrase "when acting through . . . government" deserves further commentary. The principal threat to religious liberty is not the government as such, but rather private religious sects that might, if the opportunity arose, employ the instrumentalities of government to enforce their sectarian beliefs on unwilling fellow citizens. To protect religious liberty from "government interference," as a consequence, is actually a roundabout way of protecting religious liberty from infringement by private parties.

In reality, freedom of religion needs to be protected less against the government than against the intolerant and domineering arrogance of private sects. This indirect effect of religious liberty clearly bears upon the thesis that constitutional rights protect individuals only against state action, not against private parties. Even if technically true, this legalistic claim needs to be interpreted realistically and in context: the First Amendment actually protects individual liberty from private interference through sectarian capture of government or "under color of law." A system of religious liberty must always include rules of mutual restraint that aim to prevent self-righteous citizens from making certain divisive, humiliating, and community-embittering gestures, not in all contexts, but while occupying specific roles—for instance, when acting as public-school officials. Laws that lack a secular purpose, such as those requiring the teaching of creationism in school, are unconstitutional because they give public power to private sects in a context crucial for the future peaceful coexistence of America's many religious and nonreligious groups.

As a matter of history, one of the original goals of the bar on sectarian teaching in public schools, entrenched in American constitutional law, was to shield such schools from being rent by denominational conflict. Separation between church and state helped create a common institution where socially dominant Protestants would have to learn that they could not exploit their majority status or sneer at Catholics and others as un-American. This required affirmative government efforts, in less than totally favorable circumstances, and not a policy of hands-off. It was also, incidentally, an unembarrassed attempt to legislate morality or at least to inculcate a form of moral self-restraint, which is an important aspect of morality.

The publicly funded schoolhouse was consciously fabricated as neutral territory—neutral not in the sense of free of values, but in the sense of protective of multiple convictions, remaining neutral among them. It was meant to provide an apprenticeship in coexistence, tolerance, and common action—not, of course, to teach moral skepticism or relativism. The channeling of ostensibly public resources for the educational benefit on one sect alone, by contrast, would not merely have fostered political divisions along religious lines, but would also have spoiled the implicit social pact that allows members of rival confessions in America to feel that, differences aside, they are all in the same boat and that they share a common government designed to seek out and pursue common purposes. This is the sense in which religious freedom can be seen as a social pact among churches and sects in which the government serves to some extent as a broker rather than a partner. (This is not to deny that government officials themselves benefit from cooperative relations among rival denominations.)

Religious liberty is one of the central means by which the multidenominational United States handles its inner diversity. Our pluralistic society, we might say, is held together by a division. The "barrier" between church and state has a positive, not merely a negative, function. It permits and encourages common citizenship despite religious pluralism, allowing citizens to disagree about ultimate matters while concurring on penultimate ones. Americans can disagree about "the good" (that is, the personal and religious ideals they deem worth pursuing), while agreeing about "the right" (the rules of justice that govern nonviolent coexistence and cooperation in a world of scarce resources).

Social cooperation in a heterogeneous society, including the ability to display a degree of tolerance and mutual respect, presupposes that people can put to one side their most fundamental disagreements and concur instead on more abstract or more particular matters. Citizens with different religious backgrounds and beliefs can commit themselves to religious liberty, or to the Constitution as a whole, even though the grounds supporting that commitment are quite diverse. And citizens with different religious convictions can agree on a number of particular practices from their diverse starting points. The fundamental rights of Americans can be agreed to by a heterogeneous citizenry whose adherence to common rules is supported by a wide array of attitudes and beliefs.

When acting through the state, which exercises a rough monopoly over the legitimate means of coercion, Americans are asked to put aside for the moment their conflicting religious convictions. But when acting outside state channels—through nongovernmental groups and in ordinary social contexts—they can freely act upon, or act out, their religious beliefs. Freedom of religion is far from exclusively individualistic, in other words. It necessarily includes the highly social freedoms to worship together, to preach and proselytize, and to found new churches and sects. To the extent that it involves social organization and public interaction, freedom of religion, like any other permission to act, raises the possibility of conflict among individuals and groups. And it is here that most of the public costs of maintaining religious liberty arise.

As the case of abortion reveals, religious disagreements can sometimes burst irrepressibly into public debate. But even such a seemingly irreconcilable conflict as the American abortion debate, where ultimate values are at stake, has not poisoned all social communications in America or rendered impossible the democratic resolution of other problems. The abortion controversy has been largely kept within relatively moderate bounds, for religious and unreligious Americans alike understand the delicate pact of mutual tolerance on which their polity is based. That truce or process of mutual adjustment and self-restraint, far from being demeaning, is a premise of our common life. Those committed to it are following principle as well as expediency.

Bargains are moral relationships, as well as strategic ones. That is because bargains implicitly encourage each party to see itself as a part of the whole, as only one legitimate claimant among others. According to the American social contract, when I assert my freedom of conscience, I am simultaneously affirming that all other citizens, whatever their private creed, enjoy one and the same right. This reference to reciprocity and fairness across individuals—which naturally restricts what any single individual can justifiably do or claim—is implicit in every assertion of a constitutional right under American law. Impartiality and fairness in this area not only help sustain social comity but also illustrate why it is so misleading to construe eighteenth-century rights as intrinsically selfish and antisocial.

Chapter Thirteen
RIGHTSHOLDERS AS STAKEHOLDERS

IT IS IMPOSSIBLE TO UNDERSTAND THE PLACE OF PROPERTY RIGHTS in the American social contract without asking how such rights affect those members of society who possess little or no property. How can the propertyless—to ask about the most basic form of social cooperation—be deterred from looting and burning? The criminal justice system helps safeguard accumulations of private wealth from the indignation of the poor as well as from the greed of the unscrupulous. But to protect property rights by coercive means alone, the state would have to wield frighteningly massive amounts of lethal force. Such vast and discretionary police powers would not only cost property owners dearly; it would also make them feel constantly vulnerable to rogue authorities. So the practical question, for would-be accumulators of private wealth, is how to deter theft and arson without relying exclusively on coercion.

How can the state be made strong enough to protect property rights, but not so strong that its lethally armed officers will be tempted to violate property rights for their personal enrichment? This puzzle, which touches the essence of liberalism, can be answered best by posing a second question: how can wealth be made legitimate in the eyes of poverty? Alternatively, how should the government treat the poor if one of its principal goals is to protect effectively, but with a minimal amount of abusable coercion, the property rights of the rich?

A full answer to this question would refer to publicly financed education, decent opportunities to enter the job market, the widest possible diffusion of private property, and many other state-managed allocations of collective resources. The disadvantaged will be far likelier to contribute to a common good if they believe that the privileged, too, are contributing their fair share. And a prudential approach to poverty will surely include giving the propertyless enough food from the table to prevent them from falling into rage or despair. The most ardent advocates of private property might try to ensure that everybody has some basic nourishment and shelter. Alleviating extremes of desperation among the poor may also stem from moral principles, sheer compassion, or fellow feeling, but since the castle is not safe if the cottage is starving, poverty relief sometimes emerges, perhaps most reliably, as a rich man's strategy of self-defense.

Because welfare transfers from the rich to the poor have been traditionally motivated by fear of worker radicalism, they have tended to lose middle-class support after the shrinkage of the industrial workforce and the disappearance of communism as a seemingly viable alternative to capitalism. But for owners to receive reliable protection for their property while the government obtains a steady flow of revenue, both incumbents and owners still need the cooperative self-restraint of indigent people, especially indigent young men. The underlying motivation here is easy to grasp, for, as Judge Richard Posner has remarked, "poverty in the midst of plenty is likely to increase the incidence of crime."[1] True, the wealthy can respond to this problem in a purely private manner. The moderately well-to-do can retreat into gated communities where they can effectively insulate themselves from the consequences of lower-class despair. But this is not a happy strategy even for people with money: insulation is costly, and not only in terms of dollars. If this becomes a trend, of course, social cohesion will be at risk, and it is safe to say that middle-class support for welfare programs will continue to wane.

WELFARE RIGHTS AS A SOCIAL BARGAIN

"Rights talk" in the United States is exuberantly partisan. Indeed, the political affiliations of Americans are good predictors of which rights they favor and which they disfavor. Economic conservatives want to beef up property rights while watering down welfare rights. Religious conservatives praise the right to life and condemn total separation of church and state. American Civil Liberties Union (ACLU) liberals support freedom of speech and censure the right to school prayer. Welfare-state liberals favor entitlements to public assistance and disfavor the right of companies to close plants whenever they wish.

We might even say that political positions in the United States are largely defined by the decision to propose or cherish some rights and censure others. And often arguments for or against certain rights are supported by careful arguments. But the advocate of any given right has a vested interest in making it seem that his favored right inhabits a pristine, extrahuman orbit of "law," or "the Constitution," into which bargains and clashing political values never intrude. This conceit cannot survive examination. The American rights debate is a debate about appropriate bargains and values; it is fueled by partisan passions and conflicting moral judgments and commitments. So how has

American politics nevertheless achieved the relatively consensual character upon which foreign observers so frequently remark? Could it be that the American consensus, to the extent that it exists, will survive if and only if all important social groups feel they have something to gain from mutual forbearance, that is, to the extent that each is granted some important cluster of worthwhile rights?

Even in the absence of any kind of poor relief, private ownership may engender spillover effects beneficial to the poor. Job creation is one of the most persuasive arguments in favor of private ownership publicly guaranteed. The taxation-for-protection contract, encapsulated in reliably enforced property rights, is often and accurately said to confer many palpable side benefits upon the nonrich, not only new jobs but also economic growth in general, diminished costs of subsistence goods relative to wages, and an economically vibrant counterweight to tyranny (which would inevitably harm everyone, including the poor). Moreover, the provision of opportunity and assistance to poor people always touches upon publicly shared conceptions of justice. A fair society tries to guarantee reasonable opportunities for all and also to ensure that no one drops beneath a decent floor.[2] This is part of what is meant by the central liberal idea of society as a cooperative venture.

Unless society is organized as a cooperative venture, private property as we know it cannot be created and maintained. Large American corporations could never have developed their current wealth and power without many kinds of government support. Similarly, wealthy and successful individuals owe their riches and success to social institutions that, while demanding cooperation from all, distribute rewards selectively and unequally. A capitalist economy provides the legal preconditions for the unequal accumulation of wealth. Such unequal accumulations do not fall from the sky. However hard people work, it is always an over-simplification to attribute differences of acquired wealth solely to the wealthy's "own efforts." People begin from massively different starting points, and someone born on one street in, say, Chicago, New York, or Los Angeles may have much worse life prospects than someone else born a mile away. In any case, private exertions take the form they do, and are rewarded as they are, only because of institutional arrangements that are politically chosen, administered by government and enforced through law. Arrangements that spawn unequal accumulations of wealth can certainly be justified on liberal principles, at least if they generate advantages for most. They can also be adjusted—without any offense to these principles—to ensure that some of this amassed fortune is diverted to provide minimally decent opportunities and well-being for ordinary citizens. Indeed, the very objective that justifies those arrangements—the promotion of human well-being—also argues for adjustments designed to help those who are otherwise disadvantaged. Those adjustments are part of a social bargain that, if it works well, works to the benefit of all.

Without such modest assistance, Americans born into poverty through no fault of their own might begin to interpret our social contract, whose rules they are in any case forced to obey, as a giant swindle perpetrated by the well-to-do. Something of this sort has happened before in our history. It may be happening again today.

That the rich—owing their wealth, in part, to cooperatively maintained law and government—should pay for the voluntary self-restraint and cooperation of the impoverished, rather than trying to cow them into a facsimile of self-restraint, is forcefully asserted by even the most impeccably liberal theorists. For instance, John Stuart Mill wrote that "since the state must necessarily provide subsistence for the criminal poor while undergoing punishment, not to do the same for the poor who have not offended is to give a premium on crime."[3] The right to a bottom floor of subsistence may well provide an incentive to self-discipline and cooperative behavior. There is nothing particularly eleemosynary about poor relief, when viewed from the property owner's perspective. Some forms of poor relief are compelled by abstract principles of justice. Much of it is supported by fellow feeling. But welfare benefits can also be understood as a tactical side payment to the poor attached to the original taxation-for-protection deal struck between property owners and their government.

PROPERTY RIGHTS AS A SOCIAL BARGAIN

Political scientist Theda Skocpol has argued persuasively that the American welfare state originated in the extensive system of veterans benefits that grew out of the American Civil War.[4] That welfare rights were first introduced as veterans benefits not only helps explain taxpayer willingness—at least in wartime or in the wake of war—to defray their costs. It also lends credence to the more general thesis that rights are politically stabilized as part of social bargains. It is therefore striking that, in the common-law tradition, property rights themselves originated as veterans benefits.

To simplify a complex story, William the Conqueror created property rights, as they eventually came to exist under the common law, when he distributed plots of seized lands to the Norman noblemen who had helped him overrun England. Common-law property rights, as enforceable in court, did not descend from high principle but were rather rough-hewn in a process of social give-and-take. This historical curiosity fits well with the fact that, as a matter of current legal reality, property rights, far from being rigidly fixed, remain subject to considerable renegotiation.

The enforcement of property rights in the United States is sustained partly by a mutually beneficial taxation-for-protection exchange between owners and government. Owners are willing to be taxed, to some degree, in order to have their property reliably protected against roughneck vandals and roving bandits—not to mention against deliberately kindled or accidental fire. For its part, the government is willing to refrain from imposing confiscatory tax rates, not only because of political incentives, but also because public officials understand that reliable long-term revenues will be augmented if citizens are encouraged to accumulate private wealth, keep honest books, and bank and invest their earnings inside the country, or at least within the purview and reach of the IRS. This cooperative relationship increases the security of both parties, extending their time horizons and permitting both to undertake long-term planning and long-gestation investments.

In this sense, property rights represent a selective application of public resources not only in order to encourage self-restraint on all sides—the government must refrain from confiscation and private owners must refrain from hiding their assets and acquiring property by means of force or fraud—but also to elicit new forms of creative activity, from both government and private individuals. Such socially beneficial inventiveness is unlikely to emerge under conditions where transactions and acquisitions are nerve-wrackingly insecure. Because both sides profit, the bargain can be self-enforcing and stable over time. Although the government ordinarily cannot be sued in court for failing to ensure the property rights of particular people against burglars and incendiaries, public officials who are "soft on crime" can be ousted from office.

The right to property should also be understood as an indispensable condition for democratic citizenship. The latitude, more or less broad, to accumulate private wealth is justifiable, despite the considerable inequalities it necessarily entails, partly because a decentralized and unplanned economy helps provide a reliable material basis for an unintimidated political opposition. If property can be confiscated at whim, people are not likely to have the independence and the security that will permit them to criticize the government openly. The high status of the right to property in the American system of governance reflects a general understanding that citizens can best deliberate together if their property is shielded from public officials. This is yet another way in which the right to private property serves the common good.

RIGHTS AS STRATEGIES OF INCLUSION

The prudential, as opposed to moral or humanitarian, origins of public assistance have been copiously documented. Modern public health and sanitation programs were launched in burgeoning cities because the wealthy, although they could afford the best doctors that money could buy, could not thereby protect themselves from contagious diseases ravaging the poor. Similarly, health care for workers serves the needs of employers. Regular employment and homeownership reduce the level of social instability and violent crime. Effective consumer protection can stimulate consumer demand. But by far the best reason to think of public provision as part of a social bargain is the above-mentioned origins of welfare in warfare. War in general accustoms citizens to higher tax rates, the revenues from which are then used, in peacetime, for social programs of various kinds. This development will be understandable only if we interpret welfare rights in part as bargains, as concessions granted to groups whose cooperation is necessary or desirable. In wartime, especially, property owners are confronted with their radical dependency on cooperation from the citizenry at large, especially the poor.

When those with little or no property are reluctant to fight fiercely against foreign looters and conquerors, the property rights of the rich are of little worth. For prudential reasons alone, property owners have an incentive to prevent the impoverished from feeling alienated from the polity. For their own purposes, moreover, they need to mobilize the poor, not merely sedate or placate them. To enlist the active support of the indigent, rather than merely their inert acquiescence, governments need to make palpable gestures of inclusion. Far from being negative protections from governmental interference, civil rights—such as the right to vote, the right to a fair trial, and the right to publicly subsidized education—are ways of pulling excluded individuals into the community.

A foreign example, once again, may help illustrate the way in which legal rights function to promote civic inclusion. To the great surprise and frustration of human rights workers from the

West, gypsies in Eastern Europe, whose basic survival strategy involves a scrupulous avoidance of direct contact with political authorities, often refuse to protect their rights by going to court. People who go to court, after all, must register their names, occupations, and whereabouts and provide other sensitive information to public officials. To assert one's rights is to enroll in the state's decision-making apparatus, and that is exactly what many of Eastern Europe's gypsies refuse to do. To avoid a potentially dangerous form of co-optation by public authorities, they willingly forgo their rights. They perfectly understand that constitutional rights, far from walling off a zone of private liberty beyond the reach of the state, are integral parts of a social contract on the basis of which government agencies extend their authority to virtually all sectors of social life.

Both property rights and welfare rights represent efforts to integrate differently situated citizens into a common social life. Far from eschewing all contact with government, the holders of property rights are indispensable partners of the modern liberal state. Institutionalized in memory of the last war and partly in anticipation of the next, welfare rights—involving cash transfers, medical care, food, housing, jobs, job training, or some combination of these—are one means among many to make the disadvantaged feel they, too, are participants in a shared national venture. Because all parties benefit, such a conjunction of property rights and welfare rights can be self-enforcing and stable over time.

Like wealth, poverty in America is in important ways a product of political and legal choices. Our law of property—which includes rules governing inheritance—determines who "lacks resources." Without government and law, some of the propertyless would quickly be able to procure considerable resources by private violence or stealth. That they do not do so more than they do is partly a product of legal coercion and social norms, but also of perceived mutual advantage. None of this is meant to deny that personal initiative, industriousness, thrift, and self-reliance are important virtues. Some people are poor because they lack such qualities. But if existing distributions of resources are a function of law, then a sensibly designed welfare program is a coherent part of a liberal-democratic polity, rather than an inexplicable departure from its core assumptions.

Bargains and Equality

To conceive rights as benefits funneled to citizens in exchange for political support may seem to violate the principle that rights must be impartially enforced. Do not all American citizens, even those with little of value to offer in an exchange, deserve to have, and have in fact, equal rights? After all, we do not reserve the right to a fair trial only to those who make tangible social contributions—to the healthy, say, but not to the chronically ill. And the right to vote is not restricted to the prime "stakeholders" in the country, that is to say, to property owners or those who pay hefty taxes.

Admittedly, the metaphor of bargains may seem to conflict with the moral promise of human equality. Bargaining suggests that our public authorities will prove most eager to guarantee valuable rights to those capable of rendering the government (or its incumbents) a needed service in return. To construe rights as legally enforced social bargains implies that the rich and powerful, for no convincing moral reasons, are likely to get better value from one and the same set of rights than the poor and the powerless receive. To think of rights as bargains is to expect that more prominent stakeholders will, in fact, reap larger dividends. For example, if welfare benefits represent a quid pro quo, then welfare cuts will fall most heavily on those with little political clout. In times of fiscal austerity, if rights are bargains, those who do not vote or make campaign contributions (say, recipients of food stamps) will suffer a greater loss of rights than the more influential beneficiaries of Social Security and Medicare.

While this picture is morally unappealing, it has a good deal of descriptive power. It is certainly not remote from the actual state of affairs. In societies such as the United States, which are generally and correctly judged to be free, the rich and the powerful enjoy many advantages not shared by the impoverished and the feeble, including advantages associated with the enforcement of their rights. While the rich use their private wealth to buy exquisite or tasteless luxuries, they also spend it to leverage better results from their civil liberties and basic rights than the moneyless can hope to achieve. They can hire private security personnel to improve the protection of their persons and property. They can exercise their constitutional right to have an abortion, even without government financial assistance. They can send their children to religious schools, which the indigent cannot always manage, even though the latter, too, are supposed to have their freedom of religious conscience constitutionally guaranteed. To exercise their freedom of speech the wealthiest citizens can purchase access to the mass media. To exercise their freedom to choose their public officials, they can make massive campaign contributions. And the well-off can notoriously hire the shrewdest lawyers and thus take disproportionate advantage of rights constitutionally assigned to everyone, but in a way that their less well situated fellow citizens cannot conceivably afford.

Imposing private costs—in the form, say, of user fees—is a standard way of conserving scarce resources, such as access to an institution that resolves conflicts. But screening techniques that impose private costs prevent only the poor, not the rich, from instigating frivolous appeals. True, the "contingency fee" system (whereby an attorney agrees to collect a fee only if a suit for damages turns out to be successful) is available for some cases, and it provides some poor people with the key to the courthouse. Judges also occasionally help poor litigants by awarding costs. Nevertheless, it is generally true that wealthy people derive far more than fair value from their supposedly equal rights. It would certainly be implausible to suggest that legal aid to the poor fully redresses the imbalance of resources between indigent and wealthy defendants.

This partiality of supposedly impartial rights to those endowed, for whatever reasons, with private resources is troubling. Certainly a good deal can and should be done to improve the situation, including, for example, better campaign-finance laws, better public monitoring of police abuse, and better legal services for the indigent. But a society in which private wealth could never be used to boost the use-value of "equally protected rights" would not be a free society in the way Americans use this term. To level the playing field so that all criminal defendants received roughly the same quality of legal counsel, for example, regardless of their personal assets, would require an unacceptable degree of governmental supervision and discretionary coercive control. A government capable of entirely neutralizing the influence of private resources on the value of individual rights would have to be so immensely powerful, in fact, that even the trivial misuses of its powers that would be bound to occur would probably be worse for most citizens (including the poor) than the inequalities it was ostensibly established to abolish.

The American social contract is a swindle to the extent that it leaves poor citizens below a decent floor. But helping the poor does not entail abolishing inequality. What the poor want most, after all, is not equality but help, and this they sometimes can and do receive (we continue to argue about how much and in what form) under various welfare, education, and employment programs. The effort to counteract desperate conditions, and to ensure that everyone has minimally decent life prospects, should not be confused with egalitarianism as a political creed.

Inequality of results will always be inescapable so long as rights impose private as well as public costs. Every American citizen has the right to sue the police for civil damages, but only a party with substantial private resources has a fighting chance to do so successfully. Those most likely to suffer police abuse ordinarily have no such resources and hence, in practice, enjoy no such right. Freedom of speech and the press, the right to legal counsel, the right to choose one's public officials, and even freedom of conscience are all enhanced by the superaddition of private resources to those already provided from the public budget. That the supposedly equal right to acquire private property is taken advantage of by some individuals more fully than by others does not, presumably, require extensive commentary.

But individual purchasing power is not the only source of bias in the allocation of private-law and constitutional rights in the United States. Vital public services are allocated unequally because the weak and the poor, being relatively disorganized, have too little political leverage to obtain their share of public resources. Unfortunately but inevitably, whenever money is distributed, power is likely to have some influence on who loses and who gains. Politically untouchable expenditures are usually those that provide special benefits to well-organized social groups. As government-managed services, rights are no more likely to be showered upon all citizens equally than public works are to be divvied up fairly among diverse localities with unequal lobbying power or skill. This observation is not meant to be casually cynical, however, or complacent or resigned. The dependency of rights on power does not spell cynicism because power itself has various sources. It arises not from money or office or social status alone. It also comes from moral ideas capable of rallying organized social support. Civil rights activists worked hard to mobilize support for their ideas because they unsqueamishly acknowledged that rights depend on social organization and political power. And the unquestionable contribution of the civil rights movement to the protection of civil rights for African Americans corroborates the thesis that rights reflect effective politics, and not merely the dictates of moral conscience.

"Equal protection" under a liberal regime, or at least the moral obligation to protect the rights of the weak, can have a serious and palpable meaning. But this meaning will not be discovered or made plain if we shut our eyes to the powerful inequalities of influence that pervade all societies, even liberal ones.

Chapter Fourteen
WELFARE RIGHTS AND THE POLITICS OF INCLUSION

INDIVIDUAL FREEDOM, however defined, cannot mean freedom from all forms of dependency. No human actor can single-handedly create all of the preconditions for his own action. A free citizen is especially dependent. He may feel "independent" when he goes into a do-it-yourself store and buys a do-it-yourself kit. But his autonomy is an illusion. Liberal theory should therefore distinguish freedom, which is desirable, from nondependence, which is impossible. Liberty, rightly conceived, does not require a lack of dependence on government; on the contrary, affirmative government provides the preconditions for liberty. The Bill of Rights is a do-it-yourself kit that citizens can obtain only at tax-payer-funded outlets.

On the basis of a democratically enacted statute, such as the Federal Tort Claims Act, an individual citizen may enter a court and sue the government for violating her rights. When so doing, she is acting as a free citizen even though her individual action presupposes prior state action. So a liberal nation cannot obliterate the dependency of individuals and subgroups on the state. But why should it try? Dependency of certain sorts is facilitative, not debilitating, especially if laws are democratically revisable and politicians are democratically removable from office. My right to vote or make a will depends on government provision of legal facilities serving these ends. When government declines to furnish such legal facilities (as it does, say, when it denies marriage licenses to gay couples), it is, rightly or wrongly, denying individual rights. What advances individual liberty is not nondependence on law and government, but a certain style of dependency, one that encourages personal initiative, social cooperation, and self-improvement.

Public education, provided to all, and not only on the basis of ability to pay, is only the most obvious example of affirmative state assistance, funded collectively and designed to foster individual and group self-help. Property rights have a similar purpose and result. This insight should also encourage us to redesign our regulatory and welfare programs, not in order to eliminate dependency (which is futile), but to create the kind of dependency that fosters self-help and makes it possible for most people to lead decent lives.

What Americans cherish as "independence" is actually dependence on a certain set of (liberal) institutions. I can escape the corkscrew of the local strongman—that is, be independent—only if I have the public power on my side. Empty treasuries and debilitated administrations make a mockery of paper rights. We do not have to look to foreign shores to see this point. What do we observe when we look into our poorest neighborhoods? Do indigent Americans really have the very same rights as the rest of us (freedom from unreasonable searches and seizures, protection against police abuse, the right to a fair trial), plus a wide array of welfare rights delivered at no expense to themselves? In reality, many inner-city Americans live without enforceable rights because, having been virtually abandoned by their government, they are virtually stateless.

Wealthy Americans are seldom neglected in this way. The

Americans who most genuinely "shift for themselves" are neither wealthy homeowners nor recipients of public aid, but rather
those among the homeless who eschew shelters and soup
kitchens in favor of garbage cans, subway grates, and spare
change. To say that such individuals shift for themselves is to say
that they have little access to the legal machinery that could protect them from undeserved institutionalization or from assault
by teenagers with baseball bats and gasoline cans.

Liberal governments must also prevent the disparity between
luxury and misery from growing so glaring that class hatreds
begin to threaten social stability and the regime of private property itself. One way to head off such dangers is through publicly funded education, designed to provide the means for
individual self-development and, when necessary, for escaping
desperate family conditions. But government can also respond to
the threat of tensions between haves and have-nots through various antipoverty and job-training programs. The United States's
largely successful earned income tax credit (EITC) is a good
example.[1] In addition, government can support a mortgage system with the tax code and by legally backing up the power of
private banks to evict defaulting borrowers. A well-organized
mortgage system, in turn, can spur construction and allow more
and more moderate-income families to become owner-occupants
and thereby to join the politically reliable middle class, widely
defined.

So prudence has no fundamental quarrel with morality. Welfare rights can be fair as well as expedient. To some extent, they
can be expedient only because they are perceived as basically fair.
And as anyone who has ever run an office knows, fairness is not
merely a moral norm; it is also a powerful management tool.

Without it, group morale and the inclination to pitch in will dwindle or collapse. That the same is true on a national scale is powerfully suggested by the efficiency gains in revenue collection when taxes are perceived to be roughly equitable.[2]

The obvious partiality of supposedly impartial rights toward those with private resources raises a problem of political legitimacy. Marxist writers (among others) direct our attention to this difficulty by deprecating basic rights as "merely formal," as scams perpetrated on the many, of genuine value solely to the few. All the poor person receives from capitalist democracy, allegedly, is "the right to sleep under a bridge at night." This is a gross exaggeration, but not one to be breezily dismissed. Indeed, if supposedly impartial rights accrued solely to the advantage of the rich, the American government's vital claim to represent society as a whole, rather than being a tool of special interests, would not only be tarnished. It would crumble.

The American social contract can hold only to the extent that all influential economic, racial, and religious groups believe that they are being treated with respect and rough fairness or, at least, that they are receiving a palpable return for their cooperation, collaboration, and self-restraint. Hence if one powerful sect captured the government and used it exclusively for partial or sectarian purposes, other citizens in a multidenominational country would correctly infer that an underlying social contract had been breached. And if glaring discrepancies between luxury and misery destroy the sense that all citizens are somehow in the same boat, as they threaten to do in the United States today, the government's capacity to enlist necessary social cooperation for its policies will founder.

The state's concern for political stability occasionally leads it to infringe upon otherwise constitutionally protected rights, as when the FBI employs wiretaps in response to an alleged terrorist threat. But the principal expression of the state's overriding interest in political stability is the precise balance of rights it positively protects. In an endeavor to stabilize a system of private property, the American system provides, or at least attempts to provide, the propertyless with a form of compensatory "security" that operates as a psychological equivalent to reliably enforced property rights. A democratic government cannot possibly equalize the capacity to take advantage of all the rights that it claims to guarantee. But it can modify the corrosive impression that the reliable rights "of all Americans" belong exclusively to the rich. It can do this, for example, by providing legal counsel free of charge to the indigent, by providing education for all children, and by ensuring that poor people receive food, shelter, decent health care, and employment opportunities.

At the risk of oversimplification, the public protection of the private rights of property owners can be understood as the following sort of bargain: the government first lays down, interprets, and enforces the rules that assign property to particular individuals, and then it provides security of possession to owners in exchange for political support and a steady flow of revenue. The delivery of welfare rights (understood capaciously to include more than cash transfers) is part of an ancillary exchange by which the government and the taxpaying citizens recompense the poor, or at least give them symbolic recognition, for their cooperative behavior in both war and peace. Most importantly, welfare rights compensate the indigent for receiving less value than the rich from the rights ostensibly guaranteed equally to all Americans.

Entitlement programs cost the American taxpayer $700 billion in 1996. This astronomical expenditure, which accounted for 30 percent of the budget, was not simply an expression of fellow feeling or a logical corollary of principles of justice. Rather, entitlements can be shaved back but not eliminated entirely because they lend legitimacy both to the property rights of the wealthy and to the state apparatus that enforces them. In this sense, they are a bargain among social groups in which the government of the day acts as a go-between.

Seen in this way, such rights represent an unsentimental politics of inclusion, slightly mitigating, not abolishing, the disparities of wealth incident to a liberal economy. One might even say that social welfare programs create a modern version of the ancient "mixed regime," a system that gives both poor and rich a stake. The contemporary mixed regime, however, is inscribed not in the organization of powers, as it was in ancient Rome (the Senate representing the patricians and the Tribunes representing the plebes), but rather in the expanded list of basic rights. The modern class compromise is reflected in the combination of property rights and welfare rights now characteristic not only of the United States but of all liberal-democratic regimes. Whether these rights are constitutionally entrenched, as in most European countries, or left to public policy, as in the United States, is of no particular import for the perceived value and stabilizing effect of the modern exchange of property rights for welfare entitlements.

If welfare rights in America really are granted in exchange for social cooperation, then one should expect benefits to flow to the best-organized groups among the relatively disadvantaged. One might even expect the most successful welfare programs to be those beneficial to the "middle classes." This is in fact the case. The most successful American welfare programs are organized not as bargains between classes, in fact, but as parts of an inter- generational contract among members of the middle class, broadly defined.

Most Americans spend two-thirds of their lives working. The earning cohort, through the government accountable to it, vol- untarily devotes a substantial percentage of its income to sup- porting both the young, through publicly funded education (costing many millions of dollars; precise figures are hard to obtain), and the old, through Medicare ($130 billion in 1996) and Social Security ($375 billion in 1996), programs that con- sume a large and growing share of federal revenues. This inter- generational redistribution, or system of rights, is sometimes advertised as a payback scheme, but it was never designed so that individual contributors would take out what they origi- nally put in. Instead it is a transfer plan that presupposes that the donor cohort imaginatively identifies with previous and sub- sequent generations. To keep the country going, working tax- payers swallow genuine losses in exchange for gains by the young and the old. Of course, debates go on about the appro- priate content of the Social Security system, and serious changes are currently afoot. But in its broad contours the system is stable and widely accepted, and the public support it receives is an important commentary on the moral economy of the nation.

The bargain between rich and poor in the United States, not surprisingly, is less robust. The relevant sums are far lower when poor people alone are the recipients; thus, for example, $82 bil- lion was allocated to Medicaid in 1996 and $27 billion for food stamps. Some conservatives argue that programs designed to help the poor are objectionable in principle—simply because they are funded by "takings." Others say that welfare benefits are counterproductive in practice. While the first objection makes no sense, the second must be tested empirically. Lukewarm public support for programs that target the poor alone has a further implication. While it may sound fair or prudent to restrict entitlements to the most desperately impoverished, programs that prove to be of no benefit to members of the middle class or others with political clout risk becoming extremely attractive candidates for the next round of budget cuts.

MAKING SENSE OF WELFARE RIGHTS

That free governments regularly provide public services, make selective investments, design incentives for self-discipline, and broker bargains for improving social cooperation should not be controversial. What needs stressing is that governments do all these things when enforcing rights. All governments develop techniques for handling social conflicts and eliciting social cooperation. Liberal governments typically do so by creating, assigning, and enforcing rights. As a historical matter, many basic rights enjoyed by Americans today grew out of social bargains ensuring fruitful collaboration on a national scale among highly diverse groups. This is true for religious liberty, private property, and social welfare guarantees.

Some European constitutions guarantee all citizens a right to publicly financed education up to a certain age. In practice, Americans have a similar system of guarantees, even though access here to free education is provided not by the federal government under the national Constitution but by the states. Whether or not the right to an education is guaranteed in a particular state constitution, publicly funded education is far from being an alien or anomalous presence within the political culture of the United States. It is not viewed with suspicion and dread even though it requires the government to tax and spend. It is not seen as an insult to individual agency, or as part of a cult of "victimology." Publicly funded education is simply one method among others by which the country makes long-gestation investments in the human skills necessary to keep it afloat. In this sense, investment in education closely parallels investment in the enforcement of property rights and the protection of owners from arson and acquisitive crime.

If we want to know whether or not the United States can afford investments of this kind, we should not simply examine the contents of our collective bank account. We also have to calculate the expected returns to society over the long run of spending its money this way. Taxpayers invest more or less willingly in education, just as they invest in police protection, because both are thought to pay off in the long term. Both seem worthwhile investments, among other reasons, because they increase the self-discipline and cooperative behavior of citizens and, not incidentally, expand the tax base. Education may be an intrinsic good, but it is good for instrumental reasons as well.

This good, in a liberal society, is not distributed solely according to market principles. The nation's educational efforts are not concentrated exclusively on those who are "willing to pay." We train talented young people from all ranks of society to become heart surgeons and aeronautical engineers, rather than simply auctioning off such training to the children of parents who are in a position to make the highest bid. The nation enlists talent for collective purposes wherever such talent can be found.

How can the community help the poor without making them unduly reliant on community help and discouraging their own capacity for self-improvement? The most common and persuasive criticism of the regulatory-welfare state concerns incentives to antisocial behavior and other undesirable side effects. But "dependency" in and of itself should not be considered one of them. There are different kinds of dependency, and not all of them are bad. Although police and fire protection definitely make citizens dependent on "public assistance," such paternalistic support also increases the willingness of private individuals to embellish and add to their holdings. Publicly funded education, when operating well, has the same effect. It, too, is a form of state help designed to foster self-help. The question is not how to eliminate state intervention, but how to design welfare programs to enhance autonomy and initiative.

An early example of a successful American antipoverty program was the Homestead Act of 1862, which freely distributed Western land to all settlers willing to cultivate it. The act gave legal title to 160 acres of public land to homesteaders who lived on and worked it for five years. This give-away can only be described as an example of affirmative government action. But it was a relative success (eighty million acres had already been claimed by 1900) precisely because it was a selective investment of public resources designed to foster self-discipline, long-term planning, and economic growth. Most importantly, the Homestead Act viewed the poor as producers rather than consumers. It provided individuals and families with the means and opportunity of earning their own livelihood. In this sense, it was a transfer program modeled on publicly funded education.

"Compassion with a hard edge" (to borrow British Prime

Minister Tony Blair's phrase) should be the broad principle underlying the ongoing reform of our welfare system. Rather than eliminating government assistance, we should channel public resources toward stimulating and underwriting private effort—for example, by providing business credits, financial incentives for those who hire and train low-income employees, and job training. Whenever possible, welfare recipients should be treated as potential producers, not as charity cases. The right to an education is a good model here: taxpayers provide schools, books, and teachers, but students do not simply receive benefits; on the contrary, they are required to study. That is the whole point of the idea of equality of opportunity (most reasonably understood as the provision of minimally decent opportunities for all), for the provision of opportunity is valuable only to those who seize and use it. Likewise, the government can create a right to freedom of speech, but this right is useless if people do not take the trouble to make their voices heard. The right to an education and the right to free speech (both of which require the rightsholder to act) are far better models for a reformed American welfare system than the rights of the sick, the handicapped, and the elderly, which tend to cast the rightsholder as a passive recipient of cash or services.[3] That is to say, welfare rights should resemble the right to property or the right to sue for damages, rights that provide active individuals, at the public's expense, with some of the resources they need to pursue their ends.

Compared to simple cash grants, the EITC seems to be an unusually promising initiative for this very reason. It is an entitlement designed to reward self-discipline. It is less rigid, and less inefficient, than the minimum wage.[4] Similar points can be made about child-care subsidies for working mothers and loan programs that seek to increase the incidence of home ownership among the borderline poor. While expensive, job training programs, meant to draw the unskilled into the workforce, are also promising. The point is not, however, to endorse particular reforms but to take the perspective that an understanding of the cost of rights implies: welfare rights, in effect, should be shaped on the model of classical rights—as public services, selective investments, incentives to self-discipline, and bargains meant to stimulate cooperation and stabilize productive interaction across ethnic lines.

RACE AND SOCIAL COOPERATION

In the United States, the questions raised in this book—"how much government?" "what kinds of rights?" "negative vs. positive rights?" "victimology vs. agency?" and "rights vs. responsibilities?"—are all thoroughly enmeshed with issues of race. Before the 1860s, the United States totally deprived a large swath of its population of both common-law rights and constitutional rights. Today, social programs that benefit white people, or that disproportionately benefit white people, rarely receive the level of social opprobrium reserved for programs that benefit black people or that disproportionately benefit black people. In many circles, rights are seen as having especially high costs, fiscal and otherwise, when they appear to be designed for, or mostly to be enjoyed by, African Americans.

To point this out is not to assert that programs that disproportionately benefit whites are working poorly or that those that disproportionately benefit African Americans are working well. Nor is it to imply that programs nominally designed to help African Americans actually help African Americans. The

Supreme Court's attempt to compel local school districts to operate racially integrated schools, for instance, was not a resounding success. Many critics of the regulatory-welfare state are in perfectly good faith. But their claim that "positive rights" are somehow un-American and should be replaced by a policy of nonintervention is so implausible on its face that we may well wonder why it persists. What explains the survival of such a grievously inadequate way of thinking? There are many possible answers, but inherited biases—including racial prejudice, conscious and unconscious—probably play a role. Indeed, the claim that the only real liberties are the rights of property and contract can sometimes verge on a form of white separatism: prison-building should supplant Head Start. Withdrawal into gated communities should replace a politics of inclusion.

Upon careful inspection, the current American debate seems to be less about the choice between more or less government than about the old ideal (engraved on every coin) of *e pluribus unum*. At stake is our capacity and even our willingness to live together as a nation. To assert that society is a cooperative venture, and that rights can be understood as governmentally created agreements among heterogeneous individuals and groups, is simultaneously and for the same reason to cast doubt both on libertarian fairy tales (sometimes popular among the Right and astonishingly widespread in American culture) and on "identity politics" (sometimes popular on the Left and now enjoying a powerful resurgence). To focus on the cost of rights is to urge that the collectivity define rights, and spend resources on rights, in a way that is broadly defensible to a diverse public engaged in a common enterprise.

While the cooperation and coexistence of people with varying cultural backgrounds is fundamental to the American political experiment, multiculturalism becomes a problem when it degenerates into ethnic separatism. Rights may make the problem worse if they are enforced selectively. By expending resources on some rights, or some people's rights, while stinting on others, we may promote or discourage political divisions along ethnic lines. If the rights of all Americans are perceived to be splendidly beneficial to whites, for instance, but of scant use to African Americans, then the legitimacy of our rights-enforcing regime will suffer. If the right to be free from unreasonable searches and seizures is well enforced in some communities, but a meaningless paper guarantee in others, social cohesion and stable agreements will be extremely difficult. If rights are to be seen as social bargains, generating mutual benefits and providing the terms for social cooperation, these bargains must be the sort to which, in principle, all citizens can agree.

PERSONAL RIGHTS AS COMMUNITY ASSETS

The rights of stockholders are set down in a company's bylaws or certificate of incorporation. The rights of ocean fishermen are specified in international treaties. Such rights are not natural, but conventional. They are consciously designed, in the light of experience, to coordinate mutual expectations, maximize investment, promote fairness, and encourage competent management. This is not a bad model for understanding other rights as well, including constitutional rights.

The rights of Americans are artifices created and maintained by the community with the aim of improving the quality of collective and individual life. When a nation is divided along religious, economic, or racial lines, a strategic allocation of rights can alleviate social tensions and promote social cooperation. Religious liberty allows members of rival sects, in any multidenominational society such as the United States, to participate in shared processes of democratic decision-making. Properly conceived and implemented, freedom of religion strengthens society, guaranteeing that ultimate values of this kind will not be dragged through the mud of public contestation. (Think how different our political climate would be if debate such as that over the issue of abortion were the rule rather than the exception.) Underlying agreement on general principles of social ordering—many embodied in the Constitution—and on a range of particular practices makes a common life possible despite our "multiculturalism," that is, despite deep disagreements about personal and religious ideals.[5] The privatization of religion in America allows a multidenominational society to resolve its other conflicts, those not involving ultimate values of religious conviction, by democratic compromise, fudging, and persuasion. Social coexistence and cooperation, including mutual respect, is enhanced by the protection of a private zone set aside for the exercise of freedom of religion. Taxpayers are willing to bear the costs of protecting religious liberty, not only because it helps ensure human dignity, but also because it helps keep a heterogeneous society in working order.

Other rights, too, are financed by the community at least in part because they solve difficult problems and provide widely shared benefits to the community. They are funded collectively because they are perceived to be collective goods. This is the principal reason why rights should not be opposed to duties; this is why individual liberty should not be casually associated with the corrosion of community. The contribution of rights to reconciling diverse social groups to each other, making them all feel a part of the nation and thereby encouraging public and private cooperation, is not limited to freedom of conscience. Just as important in this respect are all those rights designed to improve the conditions of relatively disadvantaged and vulnerable Americans.

When subsidizing legal services for the poor, the taxpaying public is accomplishing something concrete, but it is also making a highly visible gesture of inclusion. Welfare rights, broadly conceived, have the same purpose. This is hardly to deny that American welfare programs need to be rethought and revised. But the partisan attack on the very idea of the welfare state cannot be reasonably cast as a defense of rights in an authentic or genuine or original sense. As attention to the cost of rights makes clear, apparently nonwelfare rights are welfare rights too: public benefits designed to promote the voluntary participation of all rights wielders in society's common endeavors.

Conclusion
THE PUBLIC CHARACTER OF PRIVATE FREEDOMS

THE RIGHTS OF AMERICANS are neither divine gifts nor fruits of nature; they are not self-enforcing and cannot be reliably protected when government is insolvent or incapacitated; they need not be a recipe for irresponsible egoism; they do not imply that individuals can secure personal freedom without social cooperation; and they are not uncompromisable claims.

A more adequate approach to rights has a disarmingly simple premise: private liberties have public costs. This is true not only of rights to Social Security, Medicare, and food stamps, but also of rights to private property, freedom of speech, immunity from police abuse, contractual liberty, free exercise of religion, and indeed of the full panoply of rights characteristic of the American tradition. From the perspective of public finance, all rights are licenses for individuals to pursue their joint and separate purposes by taking advantage of collective assets, which include a share of those private assets accumulated under the community's protection.

Taking seriously the budgetary costs of all rights means loosening a number of settled convictions about the nature of American liberalism. That tax dollars must be collected before rights can be reliably enforced implies above all that individual liberty, in the United States, is more dependent upon the joint efforts of the community than is commonly acknowledged. That all rights require political officials to tax and spend suggests the speciousness of the overused distinction between positive and negative rights. That the legal rights of Americans draw on a limited pool of public resources makes clear why they can never be treated as trumps or uncompromisable claims. And finally, that rights enforcement requires public expenditures raises urgent but neglected questions of democratic accountability and distributive justice: according to what principles are tax dollars allocated for the enforcement of legal rights? And who decides how many resources are spent to subsidize which specific rights for which specific groups of individuals?

Conceived as a matter of public finance, legal rights emerge as politically created and collectively funded instruments designed to promote human welfare. Because returns from equal rights protection—such as the benefit of living in a relatively just society where, for the most part, groups with different ethnic backgrounds can peaceably coexist and cooperate—are diffuse and hard to capture, initial investments in such protection must be made by the public power.

Rights in contract law, which transform promises into binding obligations, are a model in this regard. The basic right of all Americans to enter into legally binding contracts supports habits of promise-keeping on which economic prosperity, beneficial to society as a whole, depends. Similarly, the rights to be notified, to submit evidence, to confront adverse witnesses, and so forth, are crafted to increase the accuracy of civil and criminal procedures and to decrease the risk of factual errors and mistaken decisions. Efficiency in the economy and truth in the administration of justice are public, not merely private, goods. They are secured to a substantial extent by the artful design, thoughtful allocation, reliable enforcement, and public funding of individual rights.

Like law in general, rights are institutional inventions by which liberal societies attempt to create and maintain the preconditions for individual self-development and to solve common problems, including settling conflicts and facilitating intelligently coordinated responses to shared challenges, disasters, and crises. As a means of collective self-organization and a precondition for personal self-development, rights are naturally costly to enforce and protect. As government-provided services aimed at enhancing individual and collective welfare, all legal rights, including constitutional ones, presuppose political decisions (which could have been different) about how to channel scarce resources most effectively given the shifting problems and opportunities at hand.

All of our legal rights—in constitutional law as well as private law—originally arose as practical responses to concrete problems. This is one reason why they vary over time and across jurisdictions. As instruments forged to serve evolving human interests and moral views, they are repeatedly recast, or respecified, by new legislation and adjudication. Rights also mutate because obstacles to human welfare—the problems that rights are designed to mitigate or overcome—change, along with technology, the economy, demography, occupational roles, styles of life, and many other factors.

When the need arises, state and federal lawmakers (which includes judges as well as legislators proper) have been known to recast or even abolish some traditional rights. American legislators did this, for instance, when they concluded that the best way to improve the welfare of employees and their dependents was to provide them with fixed awards in the case of on-the-job injuries. Workers' compensation statutes bar common-law remedies, that is to say, they legally extinguished the right that workers previously enjoyed to sue their employers for employ-ment-related accidents. So rights are routinely unmade as well as made. Changing impediments to human well-being and shift-ing legislative strategies effect a reconfiguration of liberty because all legal rights are, or aspire to be, welfare rights—polit-ically and judicially designed attempts to achieve human well-being in changing social contexts. When these attempts fail, as they sometimes do, rights will be, and should be, created and suspended, redesigned and reassigned.

Constitutional rights provisions, especially, contain broad and ambiguous generalities that must be interpreted and speci-fied by ever-new judicial personnel possessing moral sensibilities and commitments that vary over time. The concrete meaning of freedom of speech is not unambiguously fixed in the original text of the First Amendment, for instance, but has evolved sig-nificantly, along with both the Court and the country, during a long historical process. But rights cannot be enforced in an unchanging manner for a more mundane reason as well: enforce-ment is subject to budgetary constraints which differ from year to year. Indeed, the enforcement of rights is largely a matter of public outlays for infrastructure and skills of a legal kind. It involves, for instance, public investment in judicial salaries and real estate and auxiliary staff and in police and prison-guard training and monitoring. To take the cost of rights into account is therefore to think something like a government procurement officer, asking how to allocate limited resources intelligently while keeping a wide array of public goods in mind. Legal rights

have "opportunity costs"; when rights are enforced, other valuable goods, including rights themselves, have to be forgone
(because the resources consumed in enforcing rights are scarce).
The question is always, might not public resources be deployed
more sensibly in some other way?

This question may at first sound pettily economistic. Does
not inquiry into costs tarnish the lofty majesty of the law?
Should we consign our most precious liberties to bookkeepers or
introduce mean considerations of cost-effectiveness where ultimate vulnerabilities are involved? Should courts or other government agencies sacrifice rights simply because they are
expensive? Such apprehensions are well directed against some
forms of cost-benefit analysis, but they are misplaced when
aimed against the approach and arguments urged here.

Far from being crudely economistic, a study of the fiscal conditions of rights enforcement is fundamentally political. Attending to costs forces us to take a broad rather than a narrow view of
the public weal. It prevents us from tackling problems sequen-
tially, as they happen to catch our attention, and forces us to propose "package" solutions to a wide array of social problems.
Above all, it lays bare the indispensability of public investments, made and evaluated collectively. Rather than reflecting
a blind worship of market outcomes, that is to say, the study of
the cost of rights is meant to encourage thoughtful public policy. It is also a kind of communitarian or collectivist theme,
though with deep roots in the liberal political tradition.

The difficulties it raises are myriad, however. For one thing,
cost-consciousness in the field of rights enforcement presents a
serious challenge to the judiciary, precisely because it demands
attention to a broad range of competing demands upon the pub-

lic budget, while judges are necessarily riveted to a particular controversy, narrowly defined. Without paying serious attention to possible alternative uses of scarce taxpayer dollars, for instance, American judges regularly compel big-city governments to dole out millions of taxpayers' dollars in tort remedies. Is this a democratic and morally responsible way to expend scarce public resources? Why should this money not be spent on public education or public health?

We cannot even ask such questions, it should be noted, until we candidly acknowledge the cost of rights. The fact that American courts—the principal guardians of our most precious liberties—are poorly positioned to make intelligent allocative decisions is a reason to worry about the implications of judicial decision-making for a responsible system of public finance. But since judges are entrusted by law with the task of protecting costly rights, students of adjudication cannot reasonably ignore the cost of rights.

For in a democracy, collective expenditures should be collectively overseen. Since the enforcement of basic rights presupposes the outlay of scarce public moneys, the public is entitled to know if the game is worth the candle, if the benefits received are roughly equivalent to the expenses incurred. To the extent that it is funded by the community, a particular pattern of rights enforcement must be justified to the community, with appropriate safeguards for members of minority groups. The benefit-cost ratio must not only be positive, it must also be perceived to be positive. So should not rights enforcers—or those who hire, pay, and supervise them—be seen as financial fiduciaries? Should they not account publicly for their necessarily controversial decisions about how scarce public moneys are put to use?

Should they not make clear the principles they use when allocating benefits and burdens? And should they not explain why a chosen distribution is preferable to its feasible alternatives?

The cost of rights raises not only questions of democratic accountability and transparency in the process of allocating resources; it also brings us unexpectedly into the heart of moral theory, to problems of distributional equity and distributive justice. To describe rights as public investments is to encourage rights theorists to pay attention to the question of whether rights enforcement is not merely valuable and prudent, but also fairly allocated. The question here is whether, as currently designed and implemented, disbursements for the protection of rights benefit society as a whole, or at least most of its members, or only those groups with special political influence. Do our national priorities, in the area of rights enforcement, merely reflect the influence of powerful groups, or do they promote the general welfare? To study costs is not to shortchange politics and morality, but rather to compel consideration of such questions. The subject is so important precisely because it draws attention to the relation between rights on the one hand and democracy, equality, and distributive justice on the other.

Rights elicit public support because—and to the extent that—they permit a large collectivity of differently situated individuals to reap the substantial rewards, personal and social, of nonpredatory coexistence and mutual cooperation. To interpret rights as welfare-enhancing investments, extracted by society for society's purposes, should improve our understanding not only of the rationale for rights, but also of their inevitably redistributive character. Such a conceptualization may conceivably stimulate a richer public debate about various neglected questions, such as whether private resources (presumably extracted, in a democracy, only for public purposes publicly explained) are invested in a way that produces adequate public gains and whether these benefits and burdens are fairly shared.

PUBLIC WILLINGNESS TO PAY

To classify rights as costly public goods is not to encourage heartless policy analysts—leagued with cadres of accountants— to settle unilaterally the question of what rights citizens should or should not enjoy. On the contrary, the inevitability of trade-offs reminds us of the need for democratic control and even "civic virtue," that is, for careful taxpayer scrutiny of budgetary allocations in the area of rights protection and enforcement. Needless to say, it is much easier to call for democratic account-ability in such matters than to achieve it.

Well-trained and competent specialists have a role to play, here as elsewhere. They are indispensable for uncovering, inter-preting, and translating into easily intelligible speech the often-complex information required for meaningful public con-sultations and decision-making about rights. But experts should be on tap, not on top. Where disputable judgments of value are involved, decision-making should occur in an open and democratic fashion. Because rights result from strategic choices about how best to deploy public resources, there are good democratic reasons why decisions about which rights to protect, and to what degree, should be made in as open a man-ner as possible by a citizenry as informed as possible, to whom political officials, including judges, must address their reason-ings and justifications.

Judgments about which rights in which forms should be

granted protection and about how much social wealth should be invested in protecting these rights ought to be subject to ongoing public criticism and debate in processes of democratic deliberation. Such decisions should be guided by the basic principles of the American legal system, including, of course, those set forth in the Constitution. How judges can retain their independence while becoming more fiscally accountable presents serious and important challenges to institutional reform. But it cannot be denied that, in the United States today, important allocative decisions concerning basic rights are often made in secretive ways, with little public consultation and control. At the very least, such judgments should become publicly scrutinizable as judgments that could have been made differently and that require justification in processes of public deliberation, subject to constitutional constraints that must themselves be justified.

Justice need have no special quarrel with cost-effectiveness. No one can object to innovative methods that allow us to deliver the same level of Social Security benefits or food stamps at half the cost. No one suggests that such efficiencies undermine the moral purpose of the programs of the welfare state. The same should be said of all rights, for cost-effectiveness can be improved everywhere, including, say, in the delivery of rights protection to suspects during interrogation or to pretrial detainees. But we can begin to consider a more efficient delivery of rights protection only after we have recognized that rights have costs.

Public deliberation should therefore be focused on the following issues. (1) How much do we want to spend on each right? (2) What is the optimal package of rights, given that the resources that go to protect one right will no longer be available to protect another right? (3) What are the best formats for delivering maximum rights protection at the lowest cost? (4) Do rights, as currently defined and enforced, redistribute wealth in a publicly justifiable way? These questions have important empirical dimensions, and it is important to bring them to the fore. But their resolution depends on judgments of value as well. The empirical dimensions should be identified as such; the judgments of value should be made openly and be subjected to criticism, review, and public debate.

REDISTRIBUTION

Having barely touched upon the uses of governmental power to help the disadvantaged, this book obviously cannot conclude with a blueprint for redesigning the American welfare state. Particular judgments depend on particular facts. Like other policy initiatives, efforts to help the disadvantaged sometimes backfire. But blanket attacks on redistribution as such make little sense. Redistribution is omnipresent. It does not occur only when the government takes money from taxpayers and hands it over to the needy. Redistribution also occurs, for example, when the public force is made available, at the expense of taxpayers generally, to protect wealthy individuals from private violence and threats of violence. Even the so-called minimal state requires the extraction of private revenue for public purposes. The most dramatic example of such regressive taxation occurs when the poor are drafted into military service in wartime to defend, among other things, the property of the rich from foreign predators. Even the most minimal state redistributes resources from those "able to pay" to protect vulnerable people. In some cases, those who are protected (like the Westhampton homeowners threatened by fire) are wealthier than those who shoulder most of the burden of the protection.

Strength and weakness are not physical conditions or brute facts. The relative strength of social actors depends less on sheer muscle or raw brains than on legal institutions and entitlements and the sheer capacity for social organization and coordination. Property holders, in the late twentieth century, are comparatively strong only as a result of government support, that is, because of deftly crafted laws, enforced at public expense, that enable them to acquire and to hold onto what is "theirs." It is impossible to define who is strong and who is weak socially, therefore, without knowing on whose side political authority will stand—that is, without reference to prior decisions about the political allocation of scarce social public resources. The rich are strong because they are protected by judicially managed systems of enforceable property rights and criminal justice.

So all the troubling questions remain: are current public investments in rights enforcement wise or foolish? Are they biased or fair? In a democracy, presumably, public investments are made by the taxpaying citizenry with the anticipation of good social returns, very broadly understood. So are the returns on our investments truly good or even acceptable? Are property rights, for instance, worth what we, as a nation, spend on protecting them?

Such questions cannot be answered in the abstract, without knowing, for instance, how scarce public resources might otherwise be productively employed. But one thing is certain. The dependency of clearly defined and robustly enforced property rights on law, government, and public resources does not lessen their value. The right to private property fuels economic growth. It also lengthens the time horizons and enhances the psychological security of individual citizens, assuring them, for example, that their expressions of political dissent will not place their holdings at risk. Even though the right to private property is costly up front, it is a shrewd and even self-funding investment. (Of course, systems of private property differ among themselves, and reasonable people can disagree about the advantages and disadvantages of each. But some form of private property is an indispensable part of any well-functioning modern society.)

The right to public education can be justified in similar terms; good education is a precondition for many other things, and it has both intrinsic and instrumental value. For children, especially, rights to health care make a good deal of sense; health is valuable in itself and makes other good things possible. Thus substantial public expenditures in both areas are justified in exactly the same way as expenditures that go to the protection of private property. All such rights establish and stabilize the conditions of individual self-development and collective coexistence and cooperation.

To say that rights enforcement presupposes the strategic allocation of public resources is above all to recall how the parts fit into the whole, how liberal individualism—as opposed to the unbridled anarchism of the state of nature—presupposes a politically well organized community. Individual freedom is both constituted and bolstered by collective contributions. The cost of rights is merely the easiest to document of such contributions. Focusing on the issue of cost forces us therefore to rethink and modify the familiar but exaggerated opposition between individual and society.

American citizens can successfully protect themselves against the unwanted intrusion of society in their private affairs, but only with society's consistent support. This is true for the most self-confidently individualistic of rightsholders. For the liberty of individuals cannot be protected unless the community pools its resources and applies them in a shrewd fashion to deter and remedy violations of individual rights. Rights presuppose effective government because only through government can a complex modern society achieve the degree of social cooperation necessary to transform paper declarations into claimable liberties. Indeed, rights can be depicted as antigovernmental, as walls constructed against the state, only if the public authority's indispensable contribution to wall construction and maintenance is unjustifiably overlooked. For government is still the most effective instrument available by which a politically organized society can pursue its common objectives, including the shared aim of securing the protection of legal rights for all.

Appendix

Some Numbers on Rights and Their Costs

Although we have occasionally referred to some numbers, it has not been our purpose in this book to offer a quantitative assessment of the cost of rights. The task of producing a quantitative assessment requires acceptance of our conceptual claims, and then some further judgments, themselves complex both empirically and conceptually, about how to disaggregate various expenditures so as to come up with dollar expenditures per right. For reasons discussed in the text, it is possible to make some progress toward that task, but precise figures may be impossible to produce.

In this appendix we offer a simple table, from the 1996 *Budget of the United States,* in order to present some information on the amount spent on various activities and institutions. This information should be taken with some grains of salt, for it does not allow specification of the cost of particular rights. It does, however, give a sense of how much taxpayers spend, in federal dollars, to carry out various programs and activities and to protect various rights. The vast amount spent by the states on various aspects of rights protection are of course not included.

ACTIVITY OR INSTITUTION	DOLLARS (IN MILLIONS)
1. Operating the system of justice	
United States Courts of Appeals	303
United States Tax Court	33
District Courts	1,183
United States Sentencing Commission	9
United States Supreme Court	26
Legal Activities of Department of Justice	537
Legal Services Corporation	278
Violent crime reduction program	30
Expenses relating to U.S. prisoners	351
Court of Veterans Appeals	9
Federal prison system	2,465
2. Monitoring government	
Office of Government Ethics	8
General Accounting Office	362
Federal Election Commission	26
3. Facilitating market arrangements	
Securities and Exchange Commission	103
Federal Trade Commission	35
Animal and plant inspection	516

ACTIVITY OR INSTITUTION	DOLLARS (IN MILLIONS)
Food safety and inspection	545
Consumer Product Safety Commission	41
4. Protecting property rights	
Patent and trademark protection	82
Disaster relief and insurance	1,160
Federal emergency management	3,614
Community disaster loans	112
Management and protection of forests	1,283
Real property activities	68
Fund for rural America (agricultural support)	100
Records management connected with property	203
5. National defense	
Pay and allowances of officers in military	5,808
Pay and allowances of enlisted personnel	12,457
Pay and allowances of cadets	35
Veterans' benefits and services	3,830
Subsistence of enlisted personnel	769
Total obligations of defense department, military	20,497
6. Education	
Educational expenditures, e.g., state and local education	530

ACTIVITY OR INSTITUTION	DOLLARS (IN MILLIONS)
Elementary, secondary, and vocational education	1,369
Equal Employment Opportunity Commission	233
7. Income distribution	
Administration of food stamp program	108
Food and nutrition assistance	4,200
Social Security Administration	6,148
8. Environmental protection	
Environmental Protection Agency	41
Clean Air Act	217
Hazardous waste	159
Pesticides	64
Natural resources conservation	644
Water quality	244
9. Others	
Printing government publications	84
Postal service	85
National Archives and Records Administration	224
National Labor Relations Board	170
Occupational Safety and Health Review Commission	8
Bureau of the Census	144

NOTES

INTRODUCTION

[1] Charles Murray, *What It Means to Be a Libertarian: A Personal Interpretation* (New York: Broadway Books, 1997), p. 5; David Boaz, *Libertarianism: A Primer* (New York: Free Press, 1997), p. 12.

[2] *Budget of the United States Government, Fiscal Year 1998* (Washington, D.C.: U.S. Government Printing Office, 1997), p. 231. The 1996 budget of the Federal Emergency Management Agency ran to something over $3.6 billion (p. 1047).

[3] Enforced by informal opprobrium, rather than by legal sanction, social norms also play a role in inducing private individuals to respect each other's rights and public officials to respect the rights of private actors. Such norms do not operate independently, however; they are always enmeshed, in complex ways, with government efforts to redesign and enforce criminal law, tort law, contract law, labor law, and so forth.

[4] Not discussed here are certain hard questions about the extent to which moral considerations do or must enter into the interpretation of legal terms. See Ronald Dworkin, *Law's Empire* (Cambridge, Mass.: Harvard University Press, 1985); Frederick Schauer, *Playing by the Rules* (Oxford: Oxford University Press, 1992).

[5] Article 13 of the European Convention on Human Rights (signed in 1950 and ostensibly entered into force in 1953). The rights announced in the convention and its protocols are reliably enforced when the subscribing states treat them as part of domestic law.

[6] H. L. A. Hart, *Essays on Bentham* (Oxford: Clarendon, 1982), p. 171.

[7] Patent rights are among the few exceptions to this rule. Since the Omnibus Budget Reconciliation Act of 1990, the Patent and Trademark Office (PTO) has been required fully to fund itself through user fees. Congress allocates money to the PTO every year, but a complicated mix of paybacks (from fees collected) into the agency budget and the general budget is supposed to compensate for this up-front allocation.

[8] Under 26 U.S.C. 501(c)(3), organizations that provide legal services to promote human and civil rights are, under specified conditions, exempt from the federal income tax.

[9] U.S. Department of Justice, Bureau of Justice Statistics, *Justice Expenditure and Employment Extracts, 1992: Data from the Annual General Finance and Employment Surveys* (Washington, D.C.: U.S. Government Printing Office, 1997), Table E.

[10] Billy L. Wayson and Gail S. Funke, *What Price Justice? A Handbook for the Analysis of Criminal Justice Costs* (Washington, D.C.: Department of Justice, U.S. National Institute of Justice, August 1989).

[11] Paul A. Crotty, "Containing the Tort Explosion: The City's Case," *CityLaw*, vol. 2, no. 6 (December 1996).

[12] See Robert L. Spangenberg and Tessa J. Schwartz, "The Indigent Defense Crisis Is Chronic," *Criminal Justice*, Summer 1994; John B. Arango, "Defense Services for the Poor: Tennessee Indigent Defense System in Crisis," *Criminal Justice* (Spring 1992), p. 42 (which reports that the public defender's budget was cut by 5.3 percent); Rorie Sherman, "N.J. Shuts Down Its Advocate; Was Unique in Nation," *National Law Journal*, July 20, 1992, p. 3 (which notes that New Jersey eliminated $6 million designated to provide appointed counsel); Richard Klein and Robert Spangenberg, *"The Indigent Defense Crisis"* (report prepared for the American Bar Association Section of Criminal Justice, Ad Hoc Committee on the Indigent Defense Crisis, 1993), which reports that of the $74 billion spent on criminal justice by federal, state, and local governments in 1990, only 2.3 percent was spent on public defense nationally (pp. 1–3).

[13] *Matthews v. Eldridge*, 424 U.S. 319 (1976). Although it admitted that American taxpayers have a financial interest in getting people off the welfare rolls as soon as they are determined to be ineligible for public aid, the Court had earlier awarded those about to lose their welfare benefits a full administrative hearing *before* termination. *Goldberg v. Kelly*, 397 U.S. 254 (1970). But the Court has never dismissed the importance of cost out of hand. In *Goss v. Lopez*, 419 U.S. 565 (1975), for instance, the Court ruled that public schools could provide an extremely modest hearing to a student threatened with expulsion because "even truncated trial-type procedures might well overwhelm administrative facilities in many places and by diverting resources, cost more than it would save in educational effectiveness."

[14] This book does not address what philosophers call the "deontological" thesis that moral reasoning should be concerned with principles rather than consequences. But the cost of rights does bear on the misuse of deontological arguments

to foster illusions about the purely apolitical nature of adjudication and the non-dependence of the judiciary on the extraction and channeling of public resources. Even rights that are of intrinsic rather than instrumental worth are costly and must therefore be subject to trade-offs of some kind.

CHAPTER ONE

[1] 410 U.S. 113 (1973).

[2] 432 U.S. 464 (1977).

[3] The distinction between negative rights and positive rights should not be confused with the similar-sounding distinction between negative and positive liberty, popularized by Isaiah Berlin in *Four Essays on Liberty* (Oxford: Oxford University Press, 1969), pp. 118–172. True, negative rights and negative liberty have roughly the same meaning (freedom from interference), but positive liberty, as Berlin used the term, refers either to democratic self-government (ibid., pp. 160–63) or to human self-realization, particularly the mastery of passion by reason. "Positive rights," which Berlin did not discuss at all and which the Court, by contrast, had in mind in these decisions, refer to individual claims upon resources provided by the taxpayer and managed by the government.

[4] Among academic writers, the master taxonomist of legal rights remains Wesley Hohfeld. In his *Fundamental Legal Conceptions* (New Haven: Yale University Press, 1923), Hohfeld distinguished among permissions, claims, powers, and immunities. While interesting, this four-part schema is unsatisfactory for several reasons, including the notable fact that powers, immunities, and even permissions all involve implicit claims on governmental performance and public resources in a sense to be discussed later in this book.

[5] Liberals often cite, in this regard, T. H. Marshall's *Class, Citizenship and Social Development* (Chicago: University of Chicago Press, 1964), which identifies three phases in the evolution of British and European liberalism. Roughly speaking, civil rights developed in the eighteenth century, political rights in the nineteenth, and social rights in the twentieth. Marshall's three-part taxonomy, in other words, makes it misleadingly easy to use the negative-positive polarity to interpret Western historical development.

[6] According to Hans Kelsen, "it is always a potential plaintiff who is the subject of a right." *General Theory of Law and State* (New York: Russell & Russell, 1973), p. 83.

[7] *Budget of the United States Government, Fiscal Year 1998* (Washington, D.C.: U.S. Government Printing Office, 1997), Appendix, p. 1019.

[8] *Budget of the United States Government, Fiscal Year 1998*, Appendix, pp. 662, 1084, 1095, 1029.

CHAPTER TWO

[1] Bentham referred to such legal powers not as negative rights but as rights to "negative services." See H. L. A. Hart, "Bentham and Legal Rights," in *Oxford Essays in Jurisprudence, Second Series*, ed. A. W. B. Simpson (Oxford: Oxford University Press, 1973), pp. 171–201.

[2] *Tinker v. Des Moines School Dist.*, 393 U.S. 503 (1969).

[3] Baron de la Bréde et de Montesquieu, *The Spirit of the Laws*, trans. Thomas Nugent (New York: Hafner, 1949), Vol. I (Book XI, chap. 4), p. 150.

CHAPTER THREE

[1] Jeremy Bentham, *The Theory of Legislation*, trans. C. K. Ogden and Richard Hildreth (Oxford, Eng.: Oxford University Press, 1931), p.113.

[2] William Blackstone, *Commentaries on the Laws of England* (Chicago: University of Chicago Press, 1979), Vol. II, p. 11.

[3] *Budget of the United States Government, Fiscal Year 1998*, pp. 137 and 142–43.

[4] U.S. Department of Justice, Bureau of Justice Statistics, *Justice Expenditure and Employment Extracts, 1992*, Table E.

[5] *Budget of the United States Government, Fiscal Year 1998*, p. 246.

[6] Ibid., pp. 225–26.

[7] Ibid., Appendix, p. 395.

[8] Ibid., Appendix, p. 764.

[9] Ibid., Appendix, p. 28.

[10] Robert Ellickson, *Order without Law* (Cambridge, Mass.: Harvard University Press, 1993) shows that some forms of social ordering can occur, and do quite well, without much understanding of law and on the basis of social norms generated and followed by the relevant community. But even such a system of ordering—which is likely to be local, not national—probably depends on background norms accompanied by legal guarantees.

[11] Friedrich A. von Hayek, *The Road to Serfdom* (Chicago: University of Chicago Press, 1944), pp. 80–81.

[12] *Budget of the United States Government, Fiscal Year 1998,* Appendix, p. 1062.

[13] Ibid., Appendix, p. 1112.

[14] Ibid., Appendix, pp. 1011, 1112–13.

CHAPTER FOUR

[1] U.S. Department of Justice, Bureau of Justice Statistics, *Justice Expenditure and Employment Extracts, 1992,* Table E.

[2] *Wilson v. Seiter et al.,* 501 U.S. 294, 298 (1990).

[3] *Budget of the United States Government, Fiscal Year 1998,* Appendix, p. 689.

[4] *Bounds v. Smith* 430 U.S. 817 (1977).

[5] The Supreme Court has mentioned the possibility that "fiscal constraints" beyond the control of prison officials might "prevent the elimination of inhumane conditions," but has not explicitly ruled on "the validity of a 'cost' defense" in suits for damages under the Eighth Amendment. *Wilson v. Seiter supr.,* 301-302.

[6] *Budget of the United States, Fiscal Year 1998,* p. 670.

[7] "There is lacking that equality demanded by the Fourteenth Amendment where the rich man, who appeals as of right, enjoys the benefit of counsel's examination into the record, research of the law, and marshaling of arguments on his behalf, while the indigent . . . is forced to shift for himself." *Douglas v. People of State of California,* 372 U.S. 353 (1963).

CHAPTER FIVE

[1] *DeShaney v. Winnebago County Department of Social Services,* 489 U.S. 189 (1989).

[2] At first glance, there is much to be said for this way of thinking. Many commentators argue that the Constitution is directed "against" government intrusion, and that it does not compel government intrusion, even if the intrusion can be called protection. Of course, the First Amendment prevents state and federal governments from interfering with freedom of speech. Only by subconstitutional statutes are private organizations inhibited from doing the same. This is also true of the ban on racial discrimination. The Fourteenth Amendment's requirement of equal protection of the laws does not apply to private organizations, even to large businesses, which are required to act in a nondiscriminatory fashion by statutes, not by the Constitution.

[3] Some of the issues discussed here are dealt with in more detail in Cass R. Sunstein, *The Partial Constitution* (Cambridge, Mass.: Harvard University Press, 1993).

[4] *Shelley v. Kraemer*, 334 U.S. 1 (1948).

[5] *Edmonson v. Leesville Concrete Co.*, 500 U.S. 614 (1991).

[6] *Smith v. Allwright*, 321 U.S. 649 (1944); *Terry v. Adams*, 345 U.S. 461 (1953).

[7] *Lebron v. National Railroad Passenger Corp.*, 115 S.Ct. 961 (1995).

[8] *Burton v. Wilmington Parking Authority*, 365 U.S. 715 (1961).

[9] *Dee Farmer v. Brennan*, 511 U.S. 825 (1994).

[10] *Budget of the United States Government, Fiscal Year 1998*, Appendix, p. 670.

[11] This point is made in Richard A. Posner, *Overcoming Law* (Cambridge, Mass.: Harvard University Press, 1996), though not in his opinion for the lower court in *DeShaney*, an opinion that relied on the negative-rights/positive-rights distinction.

CHAPTER SIX

[1] "Individual rights are political trumps held by individuals." Ronald Dworkin, *Taking Rights Seriously* (Cambridge, Mass.: Harvard University Press, 1977), p. xi.

[2] Dworkin, *Taking Rights Seriously*, p. 193.

[3] *Korematsu v. United States*, 323 U.S. 214 (1944).

[4] See the discussion of exclusionary reasons in Joseph Raz, *Practical Reason and Norms*, 2d ed. (Princeton: Princeton University Press, 1993).

[5] See Jean Dreze and Amartya Sen, *India* (Oxford: Oxford University Press, 1996).

[6] So argues Leonard Levy in *Original Intent and the Framers' Constitution* (New York: Macmillan, 1988), pp. 174–220.

[7] See *Fordyce County, Georgia v. The Nationalist Movement*, 505 U.S. 123 (1992).

CHAPTER SEVEN

[1] This rough estimate is based on the debatable assumption that the cost per voter of an election is between $2 and $5. Interview with Melissa Warren, Elections Division, Secretary of State of California, July 25, 1997.

[2] Hans Kelsen, *General Theory of Law and the State* (Cambridge, Mass.: Harvard University Press, 1945), p. 88.

[3] *O'Brien v. Skinner*, 414 U.S. 524 (1974).

[4] Interview with John Cloonan, Elections Division, Secretary of the Commonwealth of Massachusetts, July 22, 1997. The city of Boston spends roughly $300,000 for each election.

[5] Interview with Melissa Warren, Elections Division, Secretary of State of California, July 25, 1997.

[6] Joseph Raz, *Ethics in the Public Domain: Essays in the Morality of Law and Politics* (Oxford: Clarendon, 1995), p. 39.

CHAPTER EIGHT

[1] Franklin D. Roosevelt, "Message to the Congress on the State of the Union" (January 11, 1944), in *The Public Papers and Addresses of Franklin D. Roosevelt* Vol. 13 (New York: Random House, 1969), p.41.

[2] Deference to the phraseology of international human rights instruments helps account for the inclusion of many prohibitively expensive rights in postcommunist constitutions. The 1966 International Covenant on Economic, Social, and Cultural Rights (now signed by 61 nations, and putatively "entered into force" in 1976) includes the right to work (Art. 6), the right of everyone to the enjoyment of just and favorable conditions of work (Art. 7), special protections for mothers and children (Art. 10), the right of everyone to an adequate standard of living and the fundamental right of everyone to be free from hunger (Art. 11), and the right of everyone to the enjoyment of the highest attainable standard of physical and mental health (Art. 12). *Twenty-Five Human Rights Documents* (New York: Columbia University Center for Human Rights, 1994), pp. 10–16.

[3] John Rawls, *Political Liberalism* (New York: Columbia University Press, 1996). Rawls refers to basic health care, employment, and a decent distribution of income, and appears to imply a right to a minimum income of some kind.

[4] B. Guy Peters, *The Politics of Taxation* (Cambridge, Mass.: Blackwell, 1991), p. 3.

[5] See John Graham and Jonathan Weiner, *Risk vs. Risk* (Cambridge, Mass.: Harvard University Press, 1996).

[6] See Stephen Breyer, *Breaking the Vicious Circle* (Cambridge, Mass.: Harvard University Press, 1993).

CHAPTER NINE

[1] *Zablocki v. Redhail*, 434 U.S. 374 (1978).

[2] See Mary Ann Glendon, *Rights Talk* (New York: Free Press, 1993).

[3] A qualification of these claims about rights and duties, not crucial to our discussion here, emerges from Joseph Raz, *The Morality of Freedom* (Oxford: Oxford University Press, 1986), pp. 183–86.

[4] For details see Richard Posner and Kate Silbaugh, *Sex Laws in America* (Chicago: University of Chicago Press, 1996).

CHAPTER TEN

[1] Thomas Hobbes, *Leviathan* (Harmondsworth, Eng.: Penguin, 1968), p. 85.

[2] The rights of union members, downstream landowners, and noncustodial parents—to be genuine rights and not merely empty phrases—presuppose well-designed systems of positive and negative incentives. The rights in question are false promises in the absence of such spurs and reins. Liberal rights, in this sense, rest not upon laissez-faire but upon a deliberate governmental sculpting of personal behavior for social ends. To claim legal rights is to act within established institutions according to well-defined rules.

[3] Alasdair MacIntyre, *After Virtue* (Notre Dame: University of Notre Dame Press, 1981).

[4] Adam Smith, *An Inquiry into the Nature and Causes of the Wealth of Nations* (New York: Modern Library, 1937), p. 98.

[5] See William Galston, "Causes of Declining Well-Being among U.S. Children," in *Sex, Preference, and Family,* ed. David Estlund and Martha Nussbaum (Oxford: Oxford University Press, 1996); Derek Bok, *The State of the Nation* (Cambridge, Mass.: Harvard University Press, 1996); David Ellwood, *Poor Support: Poverty in the American Family* (New York: Basic Books, 1988).

[6] Glendon, *Rights Talk*, p. x.

[7] Blackstone, *Commentaries on the Laws of England*, Vol. 3, p. 4. In the common-law tradition, that is to say, "rights talk" was invented to replace bully-boy talk.

CHAPTER ELEVEN

[1] The same might be said of the authors of the American Bill of Rights.

[2] U.S. Department of Health and Human Services, Office of Child Support

Enforcement, *Twentieth Annual Report to Congress for the 1995 Fiscal Year.* The American taxpayer paid one dollar for every four dollars of child support collected. (Appendix B, Table 1, p. 78).

[3] Christopher Jencks, "The Hidden Paradox of Welfare Reform," *American Prospect*, no. 32 (May–June 1997), p. 36.

CHAPTER TWELVE

[1] This exchange of rights protection for political legitimacy is one of the central themes of Jürgen Habermas, *Between Facts and Norms* (Cambridge, Mass.: MIT Press, 1996).

[2] This empirical thesis should not be confused with David Gauthier's argument that principles of justice can be defended by showing that they would have emerged from bargains based on mutual advantage, given existing distributions of talents, entitlements, and so forth. See David Gauthier, *Morals by Agreement* (Oxford: Clarendon, 1986). Philosophical arguments that invoke mutual advantage must justify, or assume the justice of, the starting point from which the bargaining parties set out. The difficulty of justifying any particular starting point is an enduring problem for those who want to use social contract theory to demonstrate the correctness of their moral conclusions. See John Rawls, *A Theory of Justice* (Cambridge, Mass.: Harvard University Press 1971); Brian Barry, *Theories of Justice* (Berkeley: University of California Press, 1989). The present chapter aims not to justify rights philosophically, but only to defend the claim that rights emerge from cooperation and enable cooperation.

[3] "This model of rights as the product of interest-driven bargains looks at least as plausible as the common notions that rights derive from mentalities, Zeitgeisten, general theories, or the sheer logic of social life." Charles Tilly, "Where Do Rights Come From?" in *Contributions to the Comparative Study of Development*, Vol. 2 ed. Lars Mjoset (Oslo: Institute for Social Research, 1992), pp. 27–28.

[4] In *Employment Division, Department of Human Resources v. Smith*, 494 U.S. 872 (1990), the Supreme Court upheld a general criminal prohibition on the religiously inspired use of peyote. The most controversial aspect of the holding was the conclusion that a neutral law, applying to all, is constitutionally unproblematic even if it has an adverse effect on religion. The Court thus read narrowly (without overruling) its prior holding in *Sherbert v. Verner*, 374 U.S. 398 (1963), which had held that unemployment compensation cannot be denied to a religious believer under a general law requiring people to seek work on Saturday. But the Court has not completely reached closure on the issue of religiously compelled exemptions from general laws. Congress attempted to overrule the *Smith*

decision by statute; the Court said that Congress lacked the power to do so, but in the process revealed an internal division on the whole question of whether (costly) exemptions may sometimes be compelled by the free exercise clause.

[5] *Employment Division, Department of Human Resources v. Smith.* See discussion in preceding note.

[6] The definition of *coercion* is no simple matter, admittedly, and religious groups are often legally permitted to be "coercive" in some possible sense of that elastic concept.

CHAPTER THIRTEEN

[1] Richard Posner, *Economic Analysis of Law*, 4th ed. (Boston: Little, Brown, 1992), pp. 463–64.

[2] See the striking empirical finding of people's judgments to this effect in Norman Frohlich and Joe Oppenheimer, *Choosing Justice* (Berkeley: University of California Press, 1993).

[3] John Stuart Mill, "Principles of Political Economy," in *Collected Works*, ed. J. M. Robson, vol. 3 (Toronto: University of Toronto Press, 1965), p. 962.

[4] Theda Skocpol, *Protecting Soldiers and Mothers: The Political Origins of Social Policy in the United States* (Cambridge, Mass.: Harvard University Press, 1992).

CHAPTER FOURTEEN

[1] See the data in Nada Eissa and Jeffrey B. Liebman, "Labor Supply Responses to the Earned Income Tax Credit," *Quarterly Journal of Economics* 111 (1996) p. 605, which shows significant increases in the workforce participation after the introduction of EITC.

[2] Margaret Levy, *Of Rule and Revenue* (Berkeley: University of California Press, 1988).

[3] Entitlements for those unable to help themselves will always be necessary, of course, especially in emergencies.

[4] A good discussion, showing vices as well as virtues in the EITC, is Daniel Shaviro, "The Minimum Wage, The Earned Income Tax Credit, and Optimal Subsidy Policy," *University of Chicago Law Review* 64, (1997), p. 405.

[5] Related themes are developed in Stephen Holmes, *Passions and Constraint* (Chicago: University of Chicago Press, 1995); and Cass R. Sunstein, *Legal Reasoning and Political Conflict* (New York: Oxford University Press, 1996).

INDEX